HEINEMANN

TEXT PROCESSING

for m... ...wards

WORD PROCESSING EXAM PRACTICE

STAGE III

S... EDWARDS

Heinemann

Heinemann Educational Publishers,
Halley Court, Jordan Hill, Oxford OX2 8EJ
a division of Reed Educational & Professional Publishing Ltd
Heinemann is a registered trademark of Reed Educational & Professional Publishing Limited

OXFORD FLORENCE PRAGUE MADRID ATHENS
MELBOURNE AUCKLAND KUALA LUMPUR SINGAPORE TOKYO
IBADAN NAIROBI KAMPALA JOHANNESBURG GABORONE
PORTSMOUTH NH (USA) CHICAGO MEXICO CITY SAO PAULO

First published 1997
2001 2000 99 98
10 9 8 7 6 5 4 3 2 1

A catalogue record for this book is available from the British Library on request.

ISBN 0 435 45388 2

Designed by Jackie Hill

Typeset by TechType, Abingdon, Oxon

Printed and bound in Great Britain by The Bath Press, Bath

Acknowledgements

I would like to thank all those who helped in the preparation of this book, particularly Rosalyn Bass at Heinemann Educational for her advice and encouragement. I would also like to thank my family – Ian, Lucy and Joseph for their help, support and patience while writing this book.

Sharon Spencer

I would like to thank Rosalyn Bass for her help and assistance in the production of this book. I would also like to thank my husband, Arthur, for his endless keying-in, proof-reading and patience.

Barbara Edwards

Contents

About this book

This examination practice book has been written to help you prepare for the Stage III RSA Text Processing Modular Awards in Text Processing and Word Processing. The book is divided into four sections.

1 Preparing for examinations

This section provides you with details of the equipment required for text processing examinations as well as hints and tips on advance preparation and how best to approach examinations. It also provides you with a list of errors which will incur faults in examinations and the opportunity to practise your proof reading skills which should be applied to any work you produce.

The Stage III Word Processing examination requires you to recall previously saved files or part of a file and make amendments as instructed. The files you will need for the word processing mock examination papers in this book are shown in this section and can be used to practise your keyboarding and accuracy skills.

2 Text Processing

This section provides details of the Text Processing Part 1 examination at Stage III and six mock examination papers to help you prepare for the examination.

3 Word Processing

This section provides details of the Word Processing Part 2 examination at Stage III and six mock examination papers to help you prepare for the examination.

Format of the book

Some of the tasks in this book may be more demanding than those you will meet in the examinations. This will help you to develop your confidence and ability to succeed in the examinations.

The letterheads and memo form for use with some of the exercises throughout this book can be found at the back of the book.

Worked examples for all the exercises are provided at the back of the book so that you can check your own work. The printed worked examples in this book are reduced by 50 per cent.

Icons

WP This icon represents mock examination papers which have been designed to be undertaken using a word processor.

T This icon represents mock examination papers which can also be undertaken using a typewriter.

Preparing for examinations

Examinations can be stressful, no matter how well prepared you are. Remembering all the equipment and stationery you will need for the examination will help you remain calm on the day. Make a list of equipment required and check this off as you get your things ready.

Check with your centre which of the following it will provide.

- Dictionary.
- Computer or typewriter manual – this may be a software manual or a centre-prepared set of notes. However, it must not contain any notes on theory.
- Ruler – showing both inches and millimetres/centimetres.
- Highlighter pen – this is useful for highlighting instructions and amendments to be made.
- Pen – for completing your answer book.
- Pencil – for writing notes such as Enc or a reminder to type a date on a letter or memo.
- Calendar – for inserting dates on letters, memos, etc. and for finding information in the text processing and word processing examinations.
- Correction pen, fluid or papers.

Advance preparation

You should try to eat something before the examination. Although you may not feel like eating beforehand, it will give you the energy to keep going. If you are hungry, you may find you become tired half-way through.

You should, of course, be on time for your examination. Try to arrive at least 15 minutes before the start time so that you can get organised. There is nothing worse than arriving late and then having to get ready quickly – this will make you feel nervous.

Make sure you understand the centre's instructions for saving your files and printing, etc. Ask questions before the examination starts to clarify these points if necessary.

If it is at all possible, have a five-minute 'warm up'. Type some paragraphs of text to get your fingers moving quickly. This will also help you calm down. Do not worry if you make lots of mistakes at this point.

During the examination

Try to have your strategy planned before the examination begins. It is helpful if you start with a short and comparatively easy task. It is not usually a good idea to start with the task containing a table. It can take a few minutes to get into the examination and so a simple task will build your confidence and help you relax. Use the time schedules given in each section of this book to see how long you should spend on each task.

You should allow around five minutes of examination time to read the instructions carefully. It is often helpful to highlight the instructions with a highlighter pen before you start a task. This will act as a checklist and you will be able to tick off the instructions as you carry them out. Make a pencil note on the examination paper to remind you of enclosures or dates that need to be inserted. Do not forget to check the examination paper carefully – there are often instructions dotted around the page.

If you do make a mistake, try not to start the task again unless absolutely necessary. Do not forget that errors such as not leaving a space between words or forgetting to indicate a new paragraph will incur only one fault. If you start the task again and then fail to complete it, you will incur many more faults.

Remember that if you attempt each task, you stand a chance of passing the examination – however, if there is a task missing, you will automatically fail. This means you must check that all tasks are clearly labelled and included in your answer book.

In your time plan allow at least ten minutes for checking your work carefully. This is probably the most important part of the examination. If you are using a word processor, one approach is to key in all the tasks and when you have finished, run each task through the spell check. This will pick up any typographical or basic spelling errors. Then, spend any time remaining checking each piece of work carefully in case you have left out a sentence or failed to carry out an instruction. Check that you have numbered any continuation pages, that you have the required number of copies and that you have used the correct stationery.

If your centre allows you to print your work during the examination, then do take advantage of this if time allows. It is often much easier to proof read printed work than check from the screen. If you are limited to the amount of paper you can use, do not forget you can print on the back of your sheets of paper. Although this is not ideal, you will only incur one fault and it is much better than not handing in a task.

Do not forget to type your full name, centre number and task number on each sheet of paper. You should complete your answer book very carefully, paying particular attention to writing your name clearly. This is where the examining board will get the information that appears on your certificate, so make sure your name is spelt correctly and is easy to read.

Good luck!

Proof reading skills

One of the most common reasons for candidates to fail examinations results from candidates not proof reading carefully enough. Once you have finished typing a piece of work, you must read it through very carefully, checking it word for word against the examination paper.

This section aims to help you improve your proof reading skills by showing you the type of errors that are commonly made in examinations. Test yourself by finding the errors in the proof reading exercises and then check them against the keys at the back of the book. This will help you develop good proof reading skills and will point out where candidates often go wrong in examinations.

Typographical and spelling errors

Typographical errors are common typing mistakes such as transposing letters within a word. For example 'hte' instead of 'the'. They are different from spelling errors and do not relate to how well a person can spell. Other examples of typographical errors include

- not having a capital letter at the beginning of a sentence (poor use of the shift key)
- not leaving a space between words (failing to hit the space bar hard enough)
- too many spaces between words or spaces within words (hitting the space bar too hard)
- additional characters within a word (pressing a key too hard or leaving your finger on a key for too long)
- omission of a character(s) within a word (pressing the key too lightly)
- capital letters within words (hitting the shift key by mistake)
- incorrect letters used (having your fingers on the wrong keys to start with)
- transposing letters (trying to type too quickly)
- numbers appearing within words (having your fingers in the wrong place).

If you notice many typographical errors in your work, it may be helpful to revise the keyboard and improve your typing technique. You do not need to go back to the beginning, just practise some typing drills each time you start to type. You only need to spend a few minutes each day on drills and you will soon notice the difference. The work you produce should become much more accurate and your typing speeds will increase.

If you are typing too quickly and are making many mistakes, then slow down a little. In the long run your work will be completed much more quickly if you do not have to go back to correct mistakes.

Spelling errors and errors of agreement

If you know that spelling is not one of your strengths, then you must check your work extra carefully. At Stage III errors are not circled. You will, however, have to learn all the abbreviations and how to spell them in full.

Once you have completed a piece of work, use the spell check facility, if you have one. This will help you to pick up any typographical errors and any obvious spelling mistakes. If there are any words that are questioned, then check carefully to ensure you choose the correct alternative. This is particularly important if your spell check uses an American dictionary. If you are unsure, then use an English dictionary. You must also check that you have typed the correct word if there are two meanings, for example, their and there.

Layout errors

There are many different layout errors that can be made. They include the following.

- Failure to date letters, memos and pre-printed forms.
- Left-hand or top margins of less than 13 mm (1/2 inch) or a ragged left-hand margin.
- No clear line space before and after separate items.
- Failure to start a new paragraph as instructed in the draft.
- Inconsistent spacing between paragraphs.
- Inconsistent use of time, money, weights, spellings, punctuation, words and figures within a document.
- Incorrect emphasis of words or sentences.
- Use of line spacing not as instructed.
- Incorrect use of stationery.
- Headings, references, etc. not as shown in the draft.
- Incorrect centring.
- Initial capitals used incorrectly – either added or omitted.
- Failure to range whole numbers or text in columns.
- Insetting of text carried out incorrectly.
- Failure to justify text as instructed.
- Incorrect adjustment of line length.
- Failure to number continuation sheets.
- Failure to indicate an enclosure(s).
- Failure to rule lines correctly (typewriting examinations).
- Failure to use the same coloured ink for drawing table lines (typewriting examinations).
- Failure to leave clear spaces above and below, right and left of lines (typewriting examinations).
- Failure to produce extra copies.
- Failure to indicate routing of extra copies.
- Failure to allocate correct amount of space as instructed in the draft.

These faults are less common than accuracy errors, but you will need to check your work carefully against the examination paper to ensure that you avoid making any of them. If you are using a word processor and can print during the examination, then you should do so. It is much easier to proof read a 'hard copy' than to check work on the screen. If you are not able to print out your work, then use the 'print review' facility so that you can see how your work looks before it is printed.

Proof Reading Practice Exercise 1

WP T

There are nine mistakes in the following document. When you have found them, type a correct version of the document and check your proof reading skills with the key and error sheet shown at the back of the book.

MEMORANDUM

To June Grove

From Richard Thomas

Ref RT/AJ

Date (Date of typing)

As term will come to an end next Friday and we begin the summer break, please insure every child in the school takes home a holiday tips sheet. In connection with older children who can be left alone at home, looking at the sheet we used last year, it needs to be updated in a number of places.

The paragraph about hot drinks needs redrafting. Include in it teaching children to use mugs and not cups as mugs our less likely to spill. They should only put as much water as they need into a kettle so that it is lightr and easier to pour. It is better to leave them a hot drink in a thermos if possible.

If they need to make a snack or meal try to leave them something cold, like sandwiches, or food that can be heated up in a microwave. Buy oven chips to avoid the use of a chippan. Use an electric Lighter for the gas to save having to use matches. Ensure children know how to use any gadget or tools they may have to use in the kitchen.

Before completing the sheet, check what holiday schems will be running in the area. Children usually enjoy the facilities they provide and our happier their than at home on there own.

Proof Reading Practice Exercise 2

WP **T**

In the following document there are twelve mistakes in the following document. When you have found them, type a correct copy of the document and check your proof reading skills with the key and error sheet shown at the back of the book.

MEMORANDUM

To Paul Masterson

From Emma Jones

Ref PM/Lunch97

Date (Date of typing)

june sales meeting lunch

As we shall have a number of special guests looking round our factory at the time of our June Sales Meeting, I thought we would take them out tolunch.

we have been sent a choice of Business Lunch Menus and have decided to choose the following, being Menu B at pounds 12.50 per head. A starter comprising mixed Hors Doeuvres followed by Aromatic Crispy Duck, Sizzling Lamb with Ginger and Spring Onions. Lemon Chicken will follow served with Stir Fried Mixed Vegetables.

I have been to the Peking Restaurant in King Street on a number of ocassions and the food has always been exellent. I have booked a table for 15 at 12 noon and hope this will be convenient for you. Please let me know by the end of next week so that I can confirm th3 numbers.

I do not think we have any vegatarians on the staff but I would be grateful if you would check on this for me and also the visitors when they arrive. I would mentioned that the Stir Fried Mixed Vegetables are almost a meal on their own? The ingredients include broccoli spears, courgettes, carrots, button mushrooms and fresh beansprouts.

We can look at the wine list when we are there.

cc

Proof Reading Practice Exercise 3

WP **T**

There are 12 mistakes in the following document. When you have found them, type a correct version of the document and check your proof reading skills with the key and error sheet shown at the back of the book.

The Flora and Fauna Conservation Society

Conservation House
Henley Road
READING
RG2 6XB

Your ref ML/J6

Our ref AS/BE

(Date of typing)

Mrs Margaret Long
Thatch College
The Green
dorchester
Dorset
DT1 8DB

Dear Mrs Margaret Long

RARE PLANTS FAIR

Thank you for your recent letter enquiring about a Rare Plants Fayre in your area. I enclose a leaflet giving all the Fairs for this year. As you will see, the nearest ones to you will be either the one at Dyrham near Bath or the one at Ashley near Tetbury.

The Fair at Dyrham will be held on Sunday 22nd June from 10.30 am to four pm. The one at Ashley Manor will be on Sat 28 June from 11 am to 5 pm.

Dyrham Park is on the A46 between Bath and the M4 Motorway. The garden has one of themost elaborate water gardens in the country. A sight well worth seeing. Ashley Manor Garden is an old fashioned one nestling up to the village church. It has a tradditional kitchen garden with herb terraces. You can find it on the A433 about 3 miles north east of Tetbury.

Whichever venue you decide to visit you will find many of the best specialist nurseries inthe country. They will be selling an enourmous range of rare plants as well as some traditional varieties.

Whether you are a beginner or a proffesional gardener you will find something of interest to you. Expert advice will be available free of charge. Teas and refreshments will be available at both Fairs.

I hope you have an enjoyable day.

Yours faithfully

Andrew Stevens
Fair Promotions

Additional text

During the Stage III Text Processing examination two additional items of information to be incorporated into document 3 will be announced. Please ensure you remember to insert the extra section in the spaces given. The additional items for document 3 of the text processing mock examination papers in this book are shown below.

WP **T** **Additional Text Exam Practice 1 Document 3**

a) Butler's Lodge is set in 50 acres.

b) The Grand Hotel has a French restaurant.

WP **T** **Additional Text Exam Practice 2 Document 3**

(a) The Directive was issued on 1 January 1990.

(b) Further information can be obtained from the Official Journal of the European Communities No L 187.

WP **T** **Additional Text Exam Practice 3 Document 3**

a) A wall thermometer is a useful way to check on how warm your rooms are.

b) Heat flows out through windows, ceilings, floors and doors.

WP **T** **Additional Text Exam Practice 4 Document 3**

a) The service will be on a trial basis of six months.

b) Problems should be referred to the Recycling Helpline on 01632 696969.

WP **T** **Additional Text Exam Practice 5 Document 3**

a) There will be five million people.

b) Use lighter shades for cushions, vases and other accessories.

WP **T**

Additional Text Exam Practice 6 Document 3

a) A cheque guarantee card and cashpoint card will be issued after three months' satisfactory banking.

b) You will require a pension of at least half your final annual salary.

Recalled text

Two of the documents in the Stage III Word Processing examination will be recalled from previously saved files for you to make amendments as instructed. Additionally, one of the documents will require you to copy *part* of a previously stored document to a specified location within a separate document.

The files you will need for the word processing mock examination papers in this book should be typed exactly as shown in the draft documents which follow. Some of the documents require you to key in text with deliberate errors for you to correct when the files are recalled – these are circled. To undertake these mock papers under examination conditions, key in the passages as shown (including the errors). When undertaking the mock examination papers the errors will appear uncircled and will need to be corrected In addition, some of the recalled text will instruct you to insert page breaks which will need to be altered when undertaking the mock examination papers

Although one of the documents requires you to copy *part* of a recalled file, the whole document should be keyed in to test your ability to recall part of a previously stored document.

Save all the files under the file name given but do not print a copy.

In the examination, these documents will be keyed in by your tutor in advance. However, when working through this book, use these documents to practise your keyboarding and accuracy skills.

Recalled Text Exam Practice 1 Document 1

WP Key in the following document exactly as shown except for line endings, which must be allowed to occur naturally. Use single-line spacing and a ragged right margin. Ensure a line length of 16 cm and insert hard page breaks as instructed. Circled text indicates a deliberate error which must be typed *as shown* (do not correct error). Save as AGENCY1.

Moving Home

Moving home is one of lifes most stressful events. Experts rate is as the third most stressful happening. It is just below the death of a spouce or divorce. Whilst it is recognised that moving home is difficult, you can take steps to ensure your move goes as smoothly as possible.

Choosing an Estate Agency

What to look for

Once you have decided to move, your first step is to register your property with an estate agent. Look in your local news paper or property paper to find some companies. Ask family and friends if they can recomend a reputable agency.

Page 2 here

Before you decide check the following

1 Does the agency advertise in the local paper regularly?
2 Are the property details they prepare, accurate and interesting?
3 Do they take colour photographs of your home?
4 Will your property details be held at each of their branches?
5 Are the staff enthusiastic and motivated?

Try to find out what other propery's the agency has sold in your area. Beware of agents who tell you they can sell your property in a very short period of time.

Page 3 here

The Valuation

It is a good idea to ask at least three local companies to value your property. Make sure that they will provide this service free of charge. This should give you a realistic idea of how much your home may fetch. It may not be the best idea to register with the agency who quotes an very high figure. This may mean your property will take a long time to sell.

Commission

Ask each agency how much commission they charge. The difference in fees between agencies can mean large savings for you. It is usual for the comission charge to be approximatly 2% - 3% of the puchase price. If you register with just one agent, and agree to keep your property with them for a specified period, they may offer a discount.

Viewings

Generally, estate agencies will not allow you to arrange viewings privately. If you see your property through a friend or relative, you will still be liable to pay your agent their commission.

Page 4 here

A good agency will be keen to arrange as many viewing as possible. Check that they will accompany prospective purchasers, particularly if you are at home alone. Make it clear that you will not receive viewers unless they have previously arranged an appointment.

Property Details

When the agent arrives to measure your property, spend some time with them discusing the best features of your home. Point out any work you have undertaken, particulary central heating, a new roof, re-wiring etc.

By following these guidelines you should be able to choose a reputable agent.

Recalled Text Exam Practice 1 Document 3

WP

Key in the following document exactly as shown except for paragraph line endings, which must be allowed to occur naturally. Use either a ragged or justified right margin. Save as AGENCY2.

ADVERTISEMENT FEATURE

PHOENIX PROPERTY AGENCY

Phoenix Property Agency has been trading successfully in this area for 21 years. Its distinctive blue and yellow signs are a familiar sight throughout the region. Phoenix signs can be seen promoting flats, houses, bungalows and even manor houses.

The Branch Manager, William Fitzgerald, stated "Phoenix Property Agency has survived the housing recession because of its caring and professional approach to selling property. We pride ourselves on our high standards of customer care."

Phoenix Property Agency has seventeen branches throughout the region and can be found in local community areas as well as high streets. Many of our branches are attached to a Phoenix Building Society for increased customer convenience.

Buying and selling property can often be fraught with difficulties. The financial help offered by Phoenix Building Society can make this difficult time much easier.

Once a property has been registered, a member of staff will visit your property to take measurements. Attractive full-colour property details are prepared and sent to all branches in the region. The details are also added to our extensive database where they will be matched with prospective buyers' requirements. Regular, full-colour advertisements are taken in local newspapers each week.

To take advantage of this marvellous deal, all you need to do is register your property for sale with Phoenix Property Agency during the month of September.

Recalled Text Exam Practice 1 Document 4

WP

Key in the following text exactly as shown except for line endings, which must be allowed to occur naturally. Use either a ragged or justified right margin. Save as AGENCY3.

When you are registering a new client it is important that they form a high opinion of Phoenix Property Agency. Ensure that a member of staff takes notes of property details as soon as possible.

The details must be typed as soon as possible and certainly no later than 3 days. The client should receive a copy to check before any are sent out.

Details must be sent to all branches in the region and to any suitable buyer on our database. This should be completed within 5 days of registering the property.

Recalled Text Exam Practice 2 Document 1

WP Key in the following document exactly as shown except for line endings, which must be allowed to occur naturally. Use single-line spacing and a ragged right margin. Circled text indicates a deliberate error which must be typed *as shown* (do not correct error). Save as HOLIDAY1.

We need to advertise and attract more people to our holidays both at home and abroad.

Our brochures for this season are now available for distribution. The opening page states how our holidays all include full board, free wine with meals, activities, entertainment and excursions. Tourists will require money to cover their own personal expenses and any optional excursions. Self-catering is an alternative.

We have a wide choice of destinations in Europe and the Med. The hotels we use range from large ones with plenty of accommodation and organised entertainment to small family-run ones with a somewhat quieter atmosphere. At most places we offer a varied programme of activities.

We need to stress the importance of these points when talking to prospective holiday-makers. Car hire is available.

Self-catering holidays are for those who wish to have a carefree break, where their time will be their own.

Please insert page break here

We have apartments in a variety of places. Whether one or two bedroom apartments, each will have a separate lounge, kitchen area and separate bathroom. The facilities in each include the following:

Crockery
Cutlery
Cooking utensils
Fridge
Iron and ironing board
Hairdryer
Linen and towels
Maid service
Telephone
Oven and cooking rings

Explain when booking these that linen and towels willbe changed each week and that all apartments have heating, gas and electricity. These are included in the price.

Please insert page break here

Coach tours at home are still very popular. All tours are accompanied by a courier and a driver. Our coaches are well upholstered for a comfortable ride. For the additional comfort of passengers, there is no smoking and no loud intrusive music on all coaches. We need to advertise for more couriers for our French tours.

New to our itinerary this year is a tour which includes a leisurely cruise for holiday-makers to enjoy. They can discover the classical sites of Greece on a tour combined with a cruise around the Greek Islands.

Special interest breaks are always well booked. Some are solidly booked for the next 2 years. This year we have added a visit to a banana plantation and botanical garden whilst on our “Gardens in Tenerife” break.

Recalled Text Exam Practice 2 Document 3

WP Key in the following document exactly as shown except for line endings, which must be allowed to occur naturally. Use either a ragged or justified right margin. Circled text indicates a deliberate error which must be typed *as shown* (do not correct error). Save as HOLIDAY2.

BOATING HOLIDAYS FOR ALL AGES

Boating holidays will appeal to all age groups. It is a relaxing and different holiday away from all the everyday cares of life. Everyone has a chance to join in.

Discover Britain along the winding rivers and canals. Cruise along these picturesque waterways at a gentle pace. Go ashore at your leisure whenever you wish and explore country side villages and historic towns. You will have opportunities to <u>fish, cycle or just walk</u> through beautiful countryside.

Select a holiday from the following parts of the country.

<u>Kennet and Avon Canal</u>

Miles and miles of idyllic boating through this conservation area. This area of water is lock-free and so you can meander along at a leisurely pace, admiring the wildlife and listening to the birdsong around you. Visit the beautiful city of Norwich with its two cathedrals and a castle.

<u>The Norfolk Broads</u>

From Bristol to London this canal will take you through rural England and give you an opportunity to experience the industrial heritage of the waterway for yourself.

Recalled Text Exam Practice 2 Document 4

WP Key in the following text exactly as shown except for line endings, which must be allowed to occur naturally. Use either a ragged or justified right margin. Save as HOLIDAY3.

On 25 December we will have a buffet lunch with party games in the afternoon. Traditional Christmas dinner will be served in the evening followed by a fancy dress ball.

On Christmas Day you will have a celebration breakfast followed by lunch. In the afternoon you can chat over tea and Christmas cake. There will be festive games in the hotel after dinner.

Christmas Day will be spent at the hotel. After a splendid Christmas lunch you will be free to watch television, read or chat among friends. After a buffet dinner you can just relax or take part in competitions organised by the hotel.

Recalled Text Exam Practice 3 Document 1

WP Key in the following document exactly as shown except for line endings, which must be allowed to occur naturally. Use single-line spacing and a ragged right margin. Ensure a line length of 16 cm and insert hard page breaks as instructed. Circled text indicates a deliberate error which must be typed *as shown* (do not correct error). Save as AUCTION1.

Auctions

Buying at an auction is great fun. You can pick up some incredible bargains. However, you must follow a few simple rules or you may end up with more than you antcipated.

To find out where the auction rooms are, look in your local news paper or phone book. Usually sales are held every month. Most towns will have at least one auction room. General household sales are the most common. These sell everything from furniture to bric a brac. Specialist sales are held less frequently, in these you will find fine art, silver, jewellery, antiques etc.

Purchasing a property through auction can often mean acquiring a property at a very realistic price. The same rules apply to property's as any other goods sold through auction. Once the hammer drops you are legally obliged to complete the purchase.

Page 2 starts here

A catalogue is usually produced for each sale. These can cost from £1 to £15 or £20 for a full colour specialist catalogue. It is worth investing in a catalogue a few days before the sale so that you can study it at your liesure.

Viewings are held a day or two before the auction and on the day itself. It is a good idea to go along and see what is on offer. If you are planning to purchase an item, check it carefully for damage or wear and tear.

On the day of the sale, try to arrive a little early. Check the items again and decide on a price that you are willing to pay for each item.

Page 3 starts here

Whatever you do, do not get carried away with the excitment of the sale and bid in excess of your reserve price.

When the bidding commences check that you can hear the auctioneer clearly. Before you enter the bidding ensure you are competing for the correct article. This sounds obvious, but you may find you end up purchasing a completley unsuitable item because you confused the catalogue numbers.

Page 4 starts here

If you are fortunate enough to make a successfull bid you will be expected to pay a deposit for your goods. This may be approximately 10% of the bid price.

This means that if you require a mortgage this must be arranged before the auction date. Discuss this with your building society manager or other mortgage lender well in advance of the auction. You will have to pay for a surveyors report and any mortgage arrangement fees in advance. A solicitor must also be appointed to carry out the Land Registry and local searches before the bidding commences.

This does mean you may incurr expenses of around £500 - £1000 and lose the purchase to another party. However, if you are successful, you must be able to pay the 10% deposit before leaving the auction rooms. You will have the satisfaction of knowing that you have purchased your home at a realistic price.

Happy bargain hunting and good luck!

Recalled Text Exam Practice 3 Document 3

WP Key in the following document exactly as shown except for line endings, which must be allowed to occur naturally. Use either a ragged or justified right margin. Save as AUCTION2.

October Sale

Household and General Items

The October sale will be held at 10 am on the first Monday of the month. Viewing will take place on the Friday and Saturday prior to the sale. The viewing times are 10.30 am - 6.00 pm Friday, 10.00 am - 2.00 pm Saturday. Catalogues are available at a cost of

These monthly sales are always well-attended as local people realise they can pick up bargains for their homes. It is advisable to arrive promptly as the saleroom is often packed to capacity.

This month, items on sale include:

Pine dressers
Sideboards
Wardrobes
Dining room table
Sofas
Washing machine
Kitchen table
Writing bureau
Dining room chairs
Piano

If you cannot attend the sale in person you can still make a bid for any of the items on sale. Leave your bid and telephone number with a member of our competent staff.

As well as the household and general items' sales we also have regular specialist auctions.

If you would like to be informed in advance of these specialist auctions then we would be delighted to do so. Write or telephone and give details of your name and address. We will ensure you receive advance notification of all our events.

Recalled Text Exam Practice 3 Document 4

WP Key in the following document exactly as shown except for line endings, which must be allowed to occur naturally. Use either a ragged or justified right margin. Save as AUCTION3.

The suitable applicant should be unflappable, extrovert and possess a sense of humour. A love of people and fine art is an absolute must. A specialist knowledge of any area of the antiques world would be a huge advantage.

As for formal qualifications, a first class degree is required. A relevant subject such as History of Art, Fine Art, etc would be useful. The successful applicant must be prepared to undertake further training.

The salary for this post will be in the region of £15,000 - £25,000 depending on experience and qualifications. However, this figure is subject to negotiation.

Recalled Text Exam Practice 4 Document 1

WP Key in the following document exactly as shown except for line endings, which must be allowed to occur naturally. Use single-line spacing and a ragged right margin. Ensure a line length of 16 cm and insert hard page breaks as instructed. Circled text indicates a deliberate error which must be typed *as shown* (do not correct error). Save as NEWHOME1.

Confidence started to return to the market last autumn. Fears of an interest rate rise to control inflationary pressures on the economy appear to have passed by. With spring just around the corner and confidence continuing in the property market, we need more new properties on our books.

It would appear that nothing that can now dampen the property market resurgence.

For months there has been an increase in the percentage of survey contributions reporting price increases with the number of sales also increasing.

Improved market conditions, together with realistic pricing has encouraged more activity in the property market.

Please insert page break here

Some areas are listed where we still have large properties forsale.

Claverton Down
Entry Hill Gardens
Abingdon Terrace
Fairfield Park
New King Street
Moorfields Road
Royal Crescent
St Catherine's Valley
The Ley
Park Street

The Ley area has a substantial 4-bedroom traditional farmhouse for sale. It has 3 reception rooms and oil central heating. Situated in an unspoilt rural position. A superb family home.

An immaculate 4-bedroom semi-detached house situated in St Catherine's Valley offers a lounge, dining hall, fitted kitchen, bathroom, separate shower room and a pleasant garden. It is in the vicinity of the village and a few minutes walk away from fields and open countryside. The perfect setting to live.

We now need to run a special promotion whilst the market is so buoyant. John Atkins will be responsible for this and he will let you have the details within the next week. Good quality, attractive literature will encourage potential buyers.

Please insert page break here

New developments continue to expand in our location. Prices range from around £40,000 to £250,000 with an average price of £60,000 for a 3-bedroom semi-detached home. There is a shortage of bungalows.

Houses at the lower end of the market are priced between £44,000 and £48,500. Depending on the location, the 2-bedroomed version, complete with parking space, would include kitchens with fitted oven and hob.

Recalled Text Exam Practice 4 Document 3

WP Key in the following document exactly as shown except for line endings, which must be allowed to occur naturally. Use either a ragged or justified right margin. Save as NEWHOME2.

A VIEW OF ST AGNES, CORNWALL

Jones and Watson are pleased to give this brief outline of the area in which Beacon View has been developed.

Local amenities include a good library, post office, two banks and a doctor's surgery. The shops in the village cater for daily provisions, clothes and footwear, pharmaceuticals, gifts and sundries.

<u>Landscape</u>

In the 18th and 19th centuries this was the bustling centre of a flourishing mining area. Although the majority

<u>History</u>

Slate and granite cottages line the main street. The coastline around St Agnes combines the freedom of the clifftops, with a lush agricultural interior. Four steep sided valleys cut into the coastline from the sea.

<u>St Agnes Beacon</u>

The Beacon is like a great island of sedimentary rock standing above the granite. Paths flanked by gorse and heather lead to the summit, which is over 600 feet above sea level. A view from here gives a 30-mile panoramic sweep of the Atlantic coast.

Village life can be fun. You will be able to take an active part in some of the Annual Events, namely the May Ball or Carnival Week in August.

Recalled Text Exam Practice 4 Document 4

WP Key in the following text exactly as shown except for line endings, which must be allowed to occur naturally. Use either a ragged or justified right margin. Save as NEWHOME3.

Whether there is a Neighbourhood Watch scheme active in the area or how far away is the local police station.

If the property is set in open countryside, are there any plans for light industrial or housing developments.

A full description of the property including outbuildings, car parking areas and gardens.

Recalled Text Exam Practice 5 Document 1

WP Key in the following document exactly as shown except for line endings, which must be allowed to occur naturally. Use single-line spacing and a ragged right margin. Ensure a line length of 16 cm and insert hard page breaks as instructed. Circled text indicates a deliberate error which must be typed *as shown* (do not correct error). Save as GOVERN1.

School Governing Board

The governing board of each local education authority maintained school is made up of a number of representatives from the school, parents and the local community.

1 Establishe the aims and policy's of the school and how the required educational standards can be met

2 Deciding how the school should be run

3 Assisting the staff to draw up the school development plan

4 Deciding how to spend the school budget in the most efficient way

5 Ensuring the National Curriculum and religious education are taught

6 Appointing a head teacher

7 Appointing, prommoting, supporting and disciplining other staff

8 Acting as a link between the school and the local community

9 Drawing up an action plan and monitoring its progress

<u>Becoming a School Governor</u>

Each school needs enthusiastic, motivated people who are intrested in the education of young children.

Page 2 here

When a vacancy arises, you can put yourself forward for election. Two parents of the children at the school must support your application. If more than one parent wishes to become a governor, an election will be held. Usually, you can write a short paragraph about yourself and your suitability to hold office. Parents are then asked to vote. The whole process should take no more than three weeks.

What Qualifications Do I Need?

Formal qualifications are not necessary, nor do you need to have any specialist knowledge of education. You will still be able to make a valid contribution to the running of a school. The head teacher and staff will be able to advice you on matters concerning education. You may be able to use your own areas of expertise in helping the school make important decisions.

What you do need is enthusiasm. It helps if you are a good listener. You will then be able to collect many different views on school issues. This will enable you to make informed decisions.

Page 3 here

Team working is another important skill. The governing board must work well together and have the schools' best interests at heart.

How much time is involved?

The full governing board usually meets twice a term. However, Committees dealing with specialised areas such as:

finance
premises
curriculum
personnel
lettings
school development
marketing

are formed and you may be expected to sit on one or two of these.

Page 4 here

As well as attending meetings you may have to read reports and Government papers and visit the school from time to time. This may not take as much time as it first appears. You do however need to make a committment to the school and be prepared to attend meetings regularly.

The board has a number of duties as well as legal responsibilities. The main duties are listed below.

Recalled Text Exam Practice 5 Document 3

WP Key in the following document exactly as shown except for line endings, which must be allowed to occur naturally. Use either a ragged or justified right margin. Save as GOVERN2.

<u>Clerk to the Governors</u>

Parker Primary School is looking for a new clerk to the governing body. The position would suit someone with school-age children as all committee meetings are held in the evenings. Parker Primary School would particularly welcome applications from parents at the school.

As well as secretarial skills, the applicant must be enthusiastic, loyal and above all, discreet. As clerk to the governing body, the post-holder will have access to a great deal of confidential information.

The most suitable candidate will have secretarial skills especially in word processing and general presentation of documents.

The duties will include attending and minuting meetings which will involve six evenings per academic term. Preparing agendas and notices, typing up minutes and distributing to the governing body will also be part of these duties.

The post-holder will also be required to deal with the routine correspondence of the governors. It is anticipated that this should not take longer than 2-3 hours per week. Liaising with the local education authority's link governor committee will also form part of this post.

An honorarium of approximately £1500 - £2000 will be paid each academic year. This is based on the post-holder working a maximum of 4 hours per week, term-time only.

1

Recalled Text Exam Practice 5 Document 4

WP Key in the following text exactly as shown except for line endings, which must be allowed to occur naturally. Use either a ragged or justified right margin. Save the document as GOVERN3.

The number of governors is dictated by the number of pupils on register. For an average sized primary school of 100 - 299 pupils, the total number of governors is 12. The maximum number must not be exceeded.

Parent governors make up four of the members, three people can be appointed by the local education authority. These generally represent local political parties. A teacher representative must also be appointed. The head teacher may choose whether they wish to be a member of the Governing Body. However, even if the head teacher decides not to be a governor, their attendance at meetings is necessary.

The Body may have up to four co-opted members. These are appointed by the Body and are usually local people who have an interest in the school. They may represent the local business community.

Recalled Text Exam Practice 6 Document 1

WP Key in the following document exactly as shown except for line endings, which must be allowed to occur naturally. Use single-line spacing and a ragged right margin. Ensure a line length of 16 cm and insert hard page breaks as instructed. Circled text indicates a deliberate error which must be typed *as shown* (do not correct error). Save as HOBBIES1.

Art, painting, sketching or calligraphy, is a wonderful way to relax. We have the unit to suit your individual need and you will find them all described in our part-time programme for this current academic year.

The pace of life today is very stressful. It is very important to use free time sensibly and follow a hobby that will give the mind and body complete relaxation.

You may have heard of our new workshop on handling conflict with creativity. Relationships at work can be damaged by conflict. This workshop uses art, visualisation and role play to identify needs and communicate feelings of anger or hurt.

Please insert page break here

The unit is suitable for people who are interested in personal growth and it requires no previous art skills. You will need to bring with you:

Cartridge paper
Adhesive tape
Collage materials
Clipboard
Crayons
Pens
Pencils
Scissors
Sketch pad

Many people have an urge to produce water-colours. They do not realise that a good background in the knowledge of drawing is imperative for final success. Many prospective students are impatient and fail to understand the need for discipline and the importance of drawing skills. Patience is a necessary skill for art work. Remember, you need confidence to be able to draw. Many people do not realise this.

Please insert page break here

If you are a beginner you can join a group and be shown how to draw a variety of objects,

Progression will take place onto the opportunity of drawing the human form as well as proportion. The group usually consists of people of all ages and abilities.

Having established the expertise necessary in drawing forms, you may wish to portray your drawing in terms of water-colour.

The more practice you have had with your pencil, the more freely you will be able to express yourself with the brush.

There are a number of courses for you to choose from. We have a structured course on colour theory and techniques of water-colour. Our syllabus allows for flexibility and does not include methodically prescribed exercises. This can be very boring and uninteresting. Room must always be left for self expression.

Recalled Text Exam Practice 6 Document 3

WP Key in the following document exactly as shown except for line endings, which must be allowed to occur naturally. Use either a ragged or justified right margin. Circled text indicates a deliberate error which must be typed *as shown* (do not correct error). Save as HOBBIES2.

CALLIGRAPHY FOR ALL

Borders with Flowers

Alphabets that will inspire everyone to design and decorate capital letters. Each alphabet is illustrated and will have basic design instructions together with ideas for variations. Whether you are interpreting the words of a text or perhaps decorating a name, your finished piece of work should be harmonious and pleasing to the eye.

Illuminated Alphabets

Artists have used plants as a source of inspiration for centuries. Delicate flower heads, stems and leaves can be safely en twined round any awkward gap or corner. Flowers can be adapted in a variety of ways. You can use a free-flowing pattern which can be lengthened or shortened as necessary. For a rose border you can decorate the initial letter, paint the inside roses in a water-colour and the bordering branches in gouache.

Colour Style

Although some traditional approaches demand the use of black ink, who can resist colour?

Colour makes calligraphy attractive, more effective and memorable.

A suitable work surface and a comfortable working position are essential for calligraphy and illumination. Use a slanting work surface. A good comfortable chair that is the right height for you will help to prevent backache.

Recalled Text Exam Practice 6 Document 4

WP Key in the following text exactly as shown except for line endings, which must be allowed to occur naturally. Use either a ragged or justified right margin. Save as HOBBIES3.

This is just one of the many weekend courses we run. Book covering and bead work are two very popular weekend courses and very quickly are fully booked.

You will be able to purchase the basic tools necessary at a cost of approximately £17.50. In addition to this there will be a charge of £12.50 for materials. The course fee will be £30 for the whole weekend.

You will be sure to enjoy your weekend away in the company of like-minded people. Everything possible is done to ensure you enjoy your creational weekend away.

Text Processing

The Stage III Text Processing Part 1 examination offered by RSA Examinations Board tests your ability to key in and lay out three business documents. You may use either a typewriter or word processor to complete the examination.

You will be asked to type three documents in one and a quarter hours. These are

1 a letter
2 a memo
3 a report or article.

You should ensure that second and subsequent pages of a document are numbered. In order to pass the examination you must complete the paper within the time given and incur no more than 17 faults. If you incur only 6 faults or less, you will be awarded a distinction.

The tasks will contain corrections and amendments for you to make. Words that need correcting will NOT be circled at Stage III. The corrections include typographical and spelling errors, punctuation and errors of agreement.

Make sure that you are familiar with the RSA list of abbreviations and spelling for Stage III.

You should ensure that you use the correct stationery. Letters must be produced on letterheads and memos on pre-printed forms. Your centre may provide you with pre-printed paper or a template on a word processor. Remember to date letters and memos with the date of the examination, include special marks as instructed and an enclosure mark as appropriate. Ensure you leave a clear line space after the printed headings before you start typing.

The letterheads and pre-printed memo form for use with the text processing mock examination papers which follow can be found on pages 108–113.

During the examination, two additional items of information to be incorporated into document 3 will be announced. You must remember to include these additional items in the spaces allocated. The additional items for the text processing mock examination papers in this book can be found on pages 10–11.

You will be asked to check a detail from one task for insertion in another. Make sure that you check this very carefully.

You will be required to add footnotes to one of the documents. You must ensure that they appear on the same page as the original footnote indication.

You must remember to use the correct measurements when inserting material and ensure that numbered items are rearranged as instructed.

One problem candidates face is running out of time in the examination. Not only must you complete the examination paper but also you should have enough time left to check your work carefully. When you are working through the mock examination papers in this section, you may like to make a note of the time each document has taken. As a guide you should aim to complete the tasks within the following time scale.

- Letter – 15 minutes
- Memo – 15 minutes
- Report or article – 30 minutes

This will allow you a total of 15 minutes to read the instructions before you type and to check through your work on completion.

Exam Practice 1 Document 1

WP T

2

Your ref GS|AC 97

Letter to Ms Gail Smithson, 55 Potterne Rd, DEVIZES, Wilts SN10 5DQ
Our ref BC|RE Please use the heading ANNUAL CONFERENCE

Mark this PERSONAL

Dr Ms Smithson
Your letter addressed to Jo White has been passed to me for attention. Jo has been absent from the dept for a number of days due to ill health and she is not expected back in the immed future.

I understand from your letter that you would like our co to provide a speaker for your Annual Conference to be held at the end of this yr.

I am ~~delighted~~ ~~pleased~~ to confirm that David Stone from our Personal Office will be delighted to attend and talk on "Dealing with Stress at Work". As the conference will be spread over 2 days, David will require accommodation at the Royal Hotel in London for the Thurs night and he will travel home on Friday evening.

I will ask him to contact you ~~Perhaps you would contact him~~ direct in conection with all other details.

Whilst looking through the outline programme for your Annual Conference I am interested to see you will have a workshop discussing the idea that "Women is Fundamental to a Successful Business". I have personally led workshops on this subject over the past few years and would be very happy to come along if you are still needing a leader. I enclose a copy of the last workshop I spoke at for your perusal.
Please contact me again if I can help in any way.

that will need to be confirmed

Yours Sncly

Barbara Cole
Chief Administrator

Exam Practice 1 Document 2

WP T

Memo from Barbara Cole to David Stone
Ref BC|RE

You will recall you said you would give a talk on "Dealing with Stress at Work" and I enclose herewith the correspondance I have received from Ms Gail S____________ in this connection ~~with a conference she is organising~~. I have said you will contact her direct concerning all details to be confurmed and I would ~~suggest~~ you do this by Friday (give date for first Friday of next month) at the latest.

Ms Smithson would like a break-down of what your talk entales. Perhaps you could give her a brief outline mentioning the main areas you will cover. For example, I know you normally include such areas' as identifying ⌊the causes of⌋ stress, what stress actually is and whether it can be bad or good for you. // I am sure you will include some case studies and how to adopt a personal coping strategy. From this will come an action plan including planning for your return to work if the stress factors have rendered you to has to have time off work for any period.

(✓) From the ~~rough sketch~~ outline programme she has sent it looks to be a very interesting conference. I have said you will need accomodation on the Thursday night but you may wish to extend your stay⁽ᴵ⁾.
Please confirm this directly with her.

I will need to have approx costings from you for this talk and the name of whom you would wish to deputise for you whilst you are away.
Please let my sec have this info.

(and travel home on the Sat)

Exam Practice 1 Document 3

WP T

CONFERENCE VENUES ← Centre this heading

Single linespacing except where indicated

Popular venues for conferences include castles converted into hotels, country houses or even floating conference facilities on board ships. We can organise the venue to suit the conference your org is arranging. Below is a description of a few of our venues.

NORTH OF ENGLAND

The Castle Hotel has 20 luxuriously appointed bedrooms and is particularly suitable for high level meetings when security and privacy are important factors. Meetings can take place in the private apartments, normally the Boardroom or library. There is also a magnificent Banqueting Hall for that all-important party at the end of the conference.

The Galaxy Centre with courtyard rooms is a specially converted conference centre comprising a mix of meeting and reception rooms. It is supported by 16 bedrooms in period cottages grouped around the Planet Courtyard.

In addition to a whole range of sporting activities, delegates can participate in clay pigeon shooting and archery.*

SOUTH EAST ENGLAND

Our converted 17th Century tith barn in Kent is a very versatile venue and includes:

This venue is particularly suitable for training courses.

1 all year round bookings
2 dinner dances
5 ~~3~~ exhibitions
3 ~~4~~ product launches
4 ~~5~~ large or small seminars
6 day or evening bookings.

Butler's Loge is an attractive early 18th Century country house set in _____ acres of w3ooded parkland. It has been tastefullly furnished with 28 elegant bedroooms and a deligh ful restaurant. The relaxed atmosphere of a large family home has been carefully maintained.

* Hot-air ballooning is another option available.

2

There are 3 specially equipped conference rooms for up to 60 delegates.

use in
For leisure time there is an open-air swimming pool within the grounds.

Please add these words from Document 1

London is your choice,
If ~~you choose London~~ we have the ______ ______ as well as other hotels for you to choose from. This hotel has 300 bedrooms furnished in period style with 2 sumptuous restaurants. There are 25 conference rooms suitable for meetings of all sizes for 20 to 250 people. It has a large indoor swimming pool, sauna, solarium and a fitness centre.

SOUTH WEST ENGLAND

This section only in double line spacing

The Grand Hotel is set in tranq1uil gardens complete with a small lake. The hotel has 50 well-appointed bedrooms and has a ______ ______ in addition to a traditional one. There are tennis courts on site and an excellent golf course in the near vicinity. Eight function rooms of varying sizes are available.

The Royal Oak, set in the centre of a 100-acre park, has 170 bedrooms and 9 meeting rooms for between 10 and 250 people. On site leisure facillities include tennis courts, bowls, croquet and a 27-hole golf course.

Water Castle is a splendid stone castle situated close to Dartmoor. It has 45 finely furnished bedrooms and there are conference facilities for up to 60 delegates. Among the liesure pursuits is pony trekking.

Emphasise this sentence

SAILING CONFERENCES

We have 3 ships for you to bear in mind if you want to organise an event with a difference.

Inset this paragraph 25mm from the left margin

You can sail to Holland, Calais, Dieppe or cruise the Irish Sea routes. Our largest ship has a 250 seat auditorium and our smallest has space for up to 50 people. You can combine lunch in Calais with a half-day programme meeting. The possibilities are endless.**

** Contact our sailing conference department for details.

All our venues are complete with the nec business aids you will need. Fax machines and photocopiers are available throughout the duration of yr booking.

Business and pleasure do go together. Leisure time is very important, that is why it is high on our list of priorities.

March 1997

2

<u>Exam Practice 2</u> Document 1

WP T

Letter to Mrs K Peterson, 50 Combe Pk, ST IVES, Cornwall TR42 1BY
Our ref MICKT/P/KP/GC
Use heading MICROSCOPE KIT

Your ref KP/sm

Mark FOR THE ATTENTION OF . . .

Dr Mrs Peterson

Thank you for yr recent letter. We are sorry to learn of yr dissappointment in are microscope kit you purchased for yr sons' birthday. // The kit is one of our most popular ~~products~~ items and we have sold over 5,000 sets this yr. As this is a high quality product we rarely rec any complaints regarding this kit and were therfore surprised to rec yr comments.

The kit was examined by ~~one of~~ a member of are staff and we agree that this particular item is faulty. The kit has now been returned to the mnfrs for there comments.

As stated in our cat, we gutee all our ~~stock~~ Merchandise will reach you in perfect conditon. Clearly we did not fulfil our gutee on this ocasion. We are therefore enclosing with this letter a cheque for eighty pounds made up as follows. The full price of the microscope kit of £65, together with a refund of five pounds for postage costs incurred in returning this product. A further £10 has been added to compensate you for the inconvenence and disappointment you have suffered. //

We hope that this incident will not prevent you form ordering from us in the future.

We look forward to hearing from you ~~soon~~.

Yrs sncly

Gary Carter
Manager

We our enclosing a copy of our latest Cat for yr perusal.

Exam Practice 2 Document 2

WP T

2

Memo from Gary Carter to Laura Paige.
Ref MICKT/P/KP/AC

Faulty Microscope kit

I attach a copy of a letter rec from Mrs P______ from which you will see, the microscope kit was in fact faulty. I has returned the kit to the mnfrs ~~for~~ and am waiting for an explanation as to how this kit past through their checking procedures.

Obviously, all the toys we sell must conform to ~~trading standards guidelines~~ toy safety regulations. The local Trading Standards Officer visits head office regularly. Any items that do not meet the rigorous safety standards are imediately withdrawn from sale.

To avoid this potentially embarassing ~~situation~~ event, please instigate a cheque on the stockroom for these kits and remove any that have the same batch no. ✓

Please issue a memo to all branch managers requesting they check their stock. Give a deadline of Monday of next week, (insert date).

Depending on the explanation rec from the mnfrs we may have to source another supplier of these items. I cannot remember seeing any microscopes at the recent trade exhibitions. Please check the latest editions of the Scientific equipment catalogues. As this is one of our best-selling items we must be sure of maintaining our stock levels.

The current trade price of the microscope kit is £35 plus VAT. Unfortunately, this is a low margin item. We cannot afford to pay more than £38 plus VAT per unit without effecting the retail price.

Exam Practice 2 Document 3

WP T

Double line-spacing except where indicated.

European Communities Commission – Directive on Toy Safety

On ——— ——— ———, a Directive was issued to ensure the same level of toy safety throughout the European Community.

Dangerous toys can be due to manufacturing errors, mechanical failure or unsuitable materials. However slight the hazard, it can cause serious injury to a small child. The safety of any toy not only depends on its manufacture, but also on its design.

Inset this paragraph 51 mm from left margin

Adults also have a responsibility to ensure children use the toys for their specific purpose. Allowing children to Mishandle ~~ing of~~ toys can turn a safe toy into a potentially hazardous item.

In order to prevent and reduce the no of accidents, each of the following groups has a part to play.

~~1~~3 The retailers
~~2~~4 The users and their carers
~~3~~1 The manufacturers
~~4~~2 The importers

Young children and babies love to smell, touch or taste different objects. This means that the materials and substances used in the mnfr of play items must be completely harmless.

The "CE" Mark

The "CE" mark or label attached to toys means that the item meets the requirements laid down in the Directive.

Importers, distributors and wholesalers must not sell toys unless they carry the CE mark. The purchaser should check the toys bear the CE mark. The manufacturers' name and address or that of their authorised representative should also be stated on the toy or packaging.

This mark must be affixed to the toy or its packaging. It must be indelible, visible and easily legible. If an item is too small for the mark to be affixed, it may be displayed on the packaging or on a separate leaflet.

Manufacturers must ensure that their products are designed and manufacturered in line with the requirements set out in the Directive. Items must conform with the standards set by the European Committee for Standardisation (CEN) and the European Committee for Electrotechnical Standardisation (CENELEC).* Conformity will provide sufficient evidence to presume that the toy has complied with the regulations of the Directive.

* These bodies set detailed technical specifications and decide test methods

2

The user also has a responsibility to ensure the toy is used as intended in accordance with the mnfrs instructions.** They must ensure that the recommended minimum age is respected and use the item in accordance with instructions.

The Member states must carry out checks on toys offered for sale and prohibit or restrict any that falsely carry the CE mark. They may also prohibit the sale of toys that are likely to endanger the health + safety of the user.

This paragraph only in single line-spacing

In the UK, the Government office responsible for these checks is the T_____ S_____ O_____.

Take this information from Document 2.

** As the user is probably a minor, then the adult resp for supervision must take this resp

Physical and Mechanical Requirements

The Directive outlines the physical and mechanical properties which toys must display if they are to qualify for the CE mark. There are a number of rules which must be adhered to.

Generally toys must be suitable for the purpose for which they were intended. They must be strong and stable enough to withstand stresses. Toys and their packaging must not present a risk of strangulation or suffication.

Chemical Requirements

As well as the physical and mechanical requirements, there are also rules on the chemical requirements of toys.

Generally they must not present any risks of poisoning or physical injury by coming into contact with the childs' skin, mucous membranes or eyes.

Flammability

All toys must be manufactured from materials that are not readily flammable.

Further info can be obtained from the O____ J____ of the E____ C____ No _____.

2

Exam Practice 3 Document 1

WP T

Your ref PM/546

Letter to Mrs P Miller, 49 Marsh St, READING RG2 8WL our ref PE/SV. Please use the heading CARING FOR THE ELDERLY

Dr Mrs Miller

Thank you for your letter recieved today asking for info on our new caring aids for the elderly. We has been working closely with various other mfrs who specialise in these aids and our work together has been very worth while.

You will see from the enclosed cat, simple ~~adaptions~~ adaptations in the home can ease pain and make life generally easier all round. Some of these simple modifications will mean life will be made easier for you too.

The following points will be useful to put to your next committee meeting. The complex you are responsible for includes rooms upstairs as well as on the level. To avoid falling over unexpected ~~objects~~ things, we recomend a well lit hall, landing and stairway with a two-way switch upstairs as well as downstairs.

Emphasise these words

As you still have baths and not showers in your rooms, ensure you have all the nec handrails fitted. These should be fixed to either walls' or the floor to ensure they give good support when getting in or out of the bath. If your committee is planning any new bathrooms, it might be better for them to consider fitting a shower unit.

This should be one that can be walked into or even allow access for a wheelchair. Special seats can also be fitted in showers, ~~so that standing for any length of time is avoided~~.

We look forward to hearing from you again.

Yours Sncly

Paul Edwards

Care Consultant

A handrail on both sides of the stairs is a must.

Exam Practice 3 Document 2

WP T

Memo from Paul Edwards to Timothy North
Ref PE|SV

Mark this URGENT

I have received the enclosed letter from Mrs M_______ in which she asks for information on our caring aids. You will note that she states that the complex she is warden for has no shower facilities. The complex are a large one on two floors with accomodation for 50 people in single rooms. At the present time there is a bathroom shared between every 4 rooms. Each single room has a wash basin only.

She is putting forward the possibility of having en suite facilities to include shower cubicles for all rooms. There is space for this work to be done without making the living area of each room too small. They will keep the ~~remaining bathrooms~~ ~~existing cloakrooms~~ but the facilities will need upgrading.

Perhaps you could look at this as a matter of urgency and go to see Mrs Miller as soon as possible. You can then discuss with her exactly what her requirments will be.

It will also be ~~that you can advise her~~ a good opp for you to advice her on the approx cost of all the work.

The existing bathrooms may only need miner adjustment's made or they may require to be completely refurbished. Look at what shelves and handrails are there. All taps will need to have lever type handles.

Try to make an appt to see her on give date for first Monday of next month.

at her next committee meeting

Exam Practice 3 Document 3

WP T

Single linespacing except where indicated

PRESERVING WINTER WARMTH ← Centre this heading

As a co working towards the well-being of the elderly we have the following hints for preserving winter warmth. These should be issued to all people living in warden controlled care, as well as those living in their own property's.

To some extent everyone is at risk [from illness] in very cold weather. Avoid taking unnecessary risks and ensure you keep warm. Food and drink are essential fuel for the body. During very cold weather, eat at least one hot meal per day and have as many hot drinks as you can. They will help to make you feel warmer inside.

Eat plenty of fresh fruit and vegetables when you are able to. Remember that bread, milk, potatoes, meat and fish* are all excellent sources of protein, vitamins and energy.

A hot drink before going to bed will help you to keep warm. Keep a vacuum flask filled with a hot drink at yr bedside as this will help if you wake up in the night feeling cold.

Other key points for keeping well and warm are:

3 ~~1~~ use draught excluders and keep curtains closed
1 ~~2~~ keep a constant temperature in all rooms
2 ~~3~~ make sure yourhome is well insulated
4 have a little exercise each day if possible
5 wrap up well before going out, wear a hat, gloves and scarf
6 keep warm in bed at night.

* Poultry, eggs, cheese and nuts are other good sources of protein.

HOME INSULATION

A comfortably warm home should be your aim at all times. At night the temperature can fall particularly low and so it is best to sleep with windows closed in cold weather. A wall ______ is a useful way to check on how warm your rooms are.

A hot water bottle is a simple and cheap way of adding extra warmth both in the day and at night. Never use a hot water bottle in bed if you have an electric blanket. Wear warm night wear and bed socks whilst in bed. (Emphasise this sentence)

A WARM HOME

All the heat in your home will eventually flow out through windows, ___ ___ ___ ___. Keep your home well insulated and draught proof where you can especially around windows. Hang a heavy curtain over the front door and get a letter box cover. (Curtains with thermal linings all help to keep draughts out.)

KEEPING ACTIVE

To aviod circulation problems, move about indoors if you are not able to get outside for some excercise. In very cold and icy weather it is bettter to stay indoors. Walk up and down stairs if you have them. This helps to exercise your whole body.

When you do go outside wear warm underwear and several ligth layers of clot5hing under your coat. WEar a scarf, gloves and a hat at all times outside.

It is also important too wear strong, warm shoes or boots. An extra pair of socks** will help if your shooes or boots are roomy enough.

(This section only in double linespacing)

** A warm insole can be added to insulate your feet against the cold.

GENERAL CARE

When having a bath [or shower,] do not take too long and avoid letting the water get cold. If taking a bath ensure it has the necessary [ ] fitted for your safety.

(Please add this word from Document 1)

Depending on your financial circumstances you may be able to get a grant to help with loft insulation and draught/proofing for doors and windows.

(Inset this paragraph 25mm from the left margin)

There are also some bu8dget schemes available for you to pay for your fuel more easily. Contact our ennergy dept for further detai;s.

March 1997

Exam Practice 4 **Document 1**

WP T

Your ref PC/LK/DO2.1

Letter to Mrs Paula Carter,
Rose Cottage, Watery Lane,
SHEPTON MALLET, Somerset
SM4 6QZ. Our ref PC/DM/63985.1
Use the heading COUNCIL RECYCLING INITIATIVE

Dear Mrs Carter

Thank you for yr recent letter expressing concern at the lack of recycling facilites in this area.

I am pleased to inform you that the local authority is just about to launch a recycling initiative in this area. Full details of this initiative will be published shortly. It could save the Counsel over £250,000 each year.

Basically, the scheme will provide for many recyclable materials to be collected from residents' homes. Special plastic boxes will be issued to each ~~home~~ household so that the materials can be seperately stored.

It is hoped that the scheme, which will be on a trail basis, will prove to be very sucessful. This does not take into a/c other benefits such as saving the energy used in the production of these materials and the conservation of natural resources. // Other measures the Environmental Commitee are considering include reducing pollution in town centres and offering a free collection service for ~~discarded~~ old refrigerators.

Out of town park and ride schemes are being built on the outskirts of the busiest town centres in the area. Public transport will ferry commutors to the centre. This service will be provided at a very small charge. It is hoped that this service will prevent commuters from bringing their vehicles into the town centre. This would reduce congestion and pollution.

I am enclosing a copy of our Enviromental Policy booklet. If you would like any further info, please let me know.

Yrs sncly
Joseph Daniels
Environmental Officer

Exam Practice 4 Document 2

WP T

Memo from Joseph Daniels to Lucy Patterson. Ref JD/LP/629.

Recycling Initiative

Mark this URGENT

I am attaching a letter I have sent to a Mrs C——. She has expressed concern at the lack of recycling facilities in the area. I hope that the scheme will be extremley successful. Mrs Carters' letter is typical of many I have rec in recent months.

We must get the publicity and promotional materials ready for the launch next month. I am attaching some notes for the leaflet that will be delivered to each ~~property~~ household. It clearly sets out how to use the collection boxes.

In order to raise awareness of this ~~programme~~ ~~initiative~~, I would like you to start planning the launch. ✓

My ideas include holding a recycling exhibision at the town hall or having a party in the park. We could also involve local school children in some way. This could be a colouring competition with the winning entray being used as a poster or leaflet design. Local traders could be approached to donate prizes for this event. It could form the cover of the recycling leaflet.

Perhaps you could consider some of these ideas and devise some of yr own. Please remeber that we has a very small budget so any events must be inexpensive to run. Let me have yr ~~comments~~ thoughts by Tuesday (give date) of next week.

Exam Practice 4 Document 3

WP T

2

Double line-spacing except where indicated.

Council Recycling Initiative ← Centre this heading

As part of the Counsel's firm committment to recycling, a collection service for reuseable materials will be set up. This new service will be on a trial basis for ________ months.

It is very much hoped that the public will respond to this important initiative. The success of our scheme relies on your co-operation.

In order to help you collect yr materials, the Council will provide you with a collection box. This will be delivered to each ~~home~~ household within the next few ~~months~~ weeks. These boxes are designed for use by an average sized household, however smaller boxes can be provided upon request.

If you do not want to ~~take part~~ participate in this scheme, ~~then~~ please contact the Council. Arrangements will be made for yr box to be collected from yr home.

All waist materials that are collected will be used for recycling. This will help conserve natural resources and reduce the energy used in mnfrg these materials. The Council estimates that over £200,000 can be saved each yr by the sail of these materials. This will benefit the whole community.

Check this detail from letter + amend if necessary

The items that can be accepted for recycling are:

1 Newspapers and magazines

2 Glass jars and bottles

~~3~~ 4 Aluminium foil

~~4~~ 5 Car batteries

~~5~~ 6 Oil filters and sump oil

~~6~~ 3 Food and drink cans

7 Clothes, shoes and rags

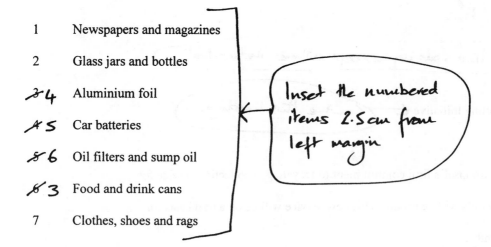

Inset the numbered items 2.5cm from left margin

It would assist our staff if you could follow these simple guidelines when leaving your waste/ materials for collection.

Newspapers and Magazines

These should be kept in a seperete bundle and placed on top of yr box. The bundle should be ~~secured~~ securely tied to prevent the papers blowing away. // Please do not include telephone directory's or cardboard.* These are not suitable for recycling.

Glass Jars + Bottles

These should be placed directly in the box. Please ensure they have been rinsed before discarding. Remove lids and corks as these cannot be used.

* A separate bank for cardboard is situated at the Avon Rd refuse tip.

Unfortunitely we cannot accept window glass or toughened glass used to make cook ware or tableware. Obviously, We cannot handle broken glass.

Emphasise these words

There is no need to separate bottles and jars into different colours.

Drink and Food Cans

We can collect steel and alumninum cans. These include drinks, food and pet food cans. Lids should be removed completely + placed inside the tin. Those with jagged edges should not be put out for collection. Please ensure that cans have been rinsed thoroughly. Dirty cans are unhygenic and ~~may~~ will cause a health hazard.

This section only in single line-spacing

Aluminium Foil

This must be placed in a sep bag.** We can only accept clean foil. Plastic or paper backed foil, ie chocolate wrappers, is not acceptable.

Car Batteries

These should be placed along side yr collection box. They should not be left outside yr property until collection day. When handling car battery's please be careful. Remember, the battery contains acid which could be harmful if spilt.

** It is helpful if you collect a full bag of foil before leaving for collection.

Oil Filters and sump Oil

Oil filters should be drained. Ensure the filter is covered in a plastic bag. This will help prevent oil leaking.

Sump oil should be placed in a clean, sealed container. Sump oil and filters should not be left on the kerbside until collection day.

Clothes, shoes and rags

Shoes should be tied together in prs. Clothes and rags should be clean. These items must be placed in a sep bag and kept dry.

If you encounter any problems with the collections, please call our R______ H______ on ______ ______.

The collections will take place each week. However, they will be on a different day to yr normal refuse collection. Bank holiday arrangements will be published in the local newspaper.

Exam Practice 5 Document 1

WP T

Your ref SW/Home

Letter to Mr Stewart Wright, 41 Empire Cres, LEAMINGTON SPA, Warwickshire CV31 2XP Our ref JM/BE Please use the heading HEARTS AND FLOWERS THEME

Dr Mr Wright

Thank you for your recent letter enquiring about our latest promotion. For the month of Feb our co will creat an easy and lively look for one of your rooms using our hearts and flowers theme. The cost will depend on the size of your room and the accessories you decide to use.

It can be very difficult to know where to ~~To know where to start is always a problem~~ begin when you is decorating a room from scratch. Our experts will advise you on which element to make your starting point. You may decide to use a colour from our range of curtain fabric as your basis to work from. This year the colours are strong. Yellow, green and blue together ~~mixed~~ with terracotta are the main ones. Many of the fabrics include the current hearts and flowers motif,

In connection with your request for info on our designs for adapting a room suitable for use as an office at home, we enclose our current cat. You will see that the essential element's are a desk, chair and storage items.

Again our experts will be able to give you ideas on the best layout for your room when they visit your home. ~~Call our Freephone number without delay~~.

You can continue the hearts and flowers theme in your office by adding heart-shaped silk or velvet cushons to your small sofa. The size of your room will dictate what furniture you will have space for.

A representative from our Design Dept will be in touch with you within the next few days.

Yours sncly

Jeremy Matthews
Sales Manager

Which is the theme for this year.

Exam Practice 5 Document 2

WP T

Memo from Jeremy Matthews to Andrew Milsome
Ref JM/BE

Mark this URGENT

We has received a good response to our Febuary promotion and I enclose a letter from Mr W______ for you to respond to. Mr Wright would like his teenage daughters' bedroom created in the hearts and flowers theme. You will need to make an appt with him to see the room and I would suggest you do this as soon as poss. The give date for the first Monday of next month would be best as I would be free to go with you.

We will need to cheque the size of the room, placement of windows and door etc. I understand Mr Wright does not wish to purchase new furniture. He only requires re-decoration, new bedliner and curtains. He is willing to by a few small accessories for the room.

The carpet is ~~pale pink~~ blush rose and as it is quite new, we will need to co-ordinate our colours around it. I foresee no problems with this job. ~~We should be able to give Mr Wright a quote on the day.~~

Whilst at the house Mr Wright would like us to look at the possibility of fitting a work station in the recess under the stares. He would like one that can be disguised as a cupboard when not in use.

We will need to have an idea of the approx cost of this before we go.

Exam Practice 5 Document 3

WP T

2

HOME IMPROVEMENT AND DECORATION

Centre this heading

Double linespacing except where indicated

More and more people are going to work without actuallly stepping outside the door. By the beginning of the next century it is estimated that over ____ million people will be working from home. The three essential elements needed are a desk, chiar and storage equipment.

FURNITURE

You should be able to sit comfortably at your desk with your knees under it. Some have drawers to one side which are useful for storage space.*

Your desk should suit the equipment you will be using. A desk space arranged in an L-shape would be best if you have a computer, a fax, telephone and other misc items. ~~Make sure~~ It is nec to have your desk near a natural source of light and your computer at an angle to the window to reduce the glare.

Never compromise by making do with a chair from the dining room. Your ideal chair should include the following:

3 ~~1~~ adjustable seat

1 ~~2~~ lumber support to avoid back pains

2 ~~3~~ swivel action for easy move ment

4 arm supports

5 castors to avoid over strething

6 hieght adjustment.

* Trestle tables are a cheaper alternative to desks.

Organise an efficient filing system before you have papers piling up. Have the things you use most frequently close at hand. Consider what you have to store and put papers in filing boxes or a filing cabinet. Shelves or drawers are useful storage for other things.

ROOM BLENDING

Many furniture desiners are realising that space is at a premium in most homes. Office furniture may end up in a room that is reglarly used by the family. For this reason it is very import5ant that it should blend in with the existing surroundings.

The dining room and the guest room are the most popular places to set up a home office as these room aer not usually in constant use. Choose a desk and chair that blend or co-ordinate with your existing decoration.

Emphasise these words only

Cover any files or binders with a fabric to match your curtains. Use a screen to hide your office furniture. You could cover the screen in a fabric to match your room.

This section only in single linespacing

and this would be an ideal way of screening off your work area

DECORATION

You can create your own office in an alcove or even a recess under the stairs. Divide your largest room into two sections using versatile backless book shelves.**
Use roller blinds or sliding doors to close off office space in alcoves and recesses when not in use.

MAKING SPACE

All the very strong colours are very popular this yr. As well as yellow, green and blue you can choose the colour ________ (please insert this colour from Document 1) to have as a textured cover for your soft furnishings. The overall effect of bold colours makes a strong statement to your room. Use lighter shades for cushions, vases and ______ ______. Choose pastel shades for walls and ceiling if using bold colours for furniture.

(Inset this section 25mm from the left margin)

February, being traditionally known as the romantic month of the year, is the time to decorate using pastel shades. A combination of pale blue and white can bring a touch of romance to a room. White voile cross-over curtains filter the light at a window. Scattered rose design bed linen and rose gingham drapes all add to the effect. Heart-shaped picture frames and mirrors or clocks are the ideal accessories.

Flowers add the final touch to any room. During spring, tulips are the most colourful and varied seasona; flower around. They are easy to work with and make wonderful arrangements.

March 1997

** These can be combined to create numerous shapes.

Exam Practice 6 Document 1

WP T

Letter to Mr C Norris
51 Battlefield Hill Road
HASTINGS E Sussex HT1 3QD
Our ref CN/AD/139.6.2
Please use the heading BANKING SERVICES

Your ref BM/CR

Dr Mr Norris

Thank you for yr recent letter enquiring about our banking services. I am pleased to enclose a copy of our brochure entitled 'Banking in the 90s. This brochure contains detailed explainations of all our banking services. // I gather from yr letter that you are disatisfied with yr the level of customer service provided by yr currant bankers. We pride ourselfs on our excellent customer service at Grange Bank plc. All our staff are fully trained in all aspects of our range of products and services. When you join our bank You can call them direct with any problem or query you may have.

Ⓥ The law ~~dictates~~ says that any financal advise we give must remain impartial. We feel we offer the best independent financial advice around.

We have our own stockbrokers, mortgage consultants and insurance brokers who will be pleased to discuss any aspect of there specialist areas with you. Should you decide to place yr bus with us/ you will be assigned to a personal banker after talking to our specialists, you can be assured of a fast, proffessional service. //

Please take the time to read our brochure. ~~It is full of useful info~~. We are sure you will be impressed ~~by~~ with the range of products and services we offer. If, after reading our literature, you require any further info, please do not hesitate to contact me.

Yrs sncly

Andrew Dalton
Branch Manager

Exam Practice 6 Document 2

WP **T**

Memo from Andrew Dalton to Martin Winters
Ref CP/AD/1396.1

Mark this CONFIDENTIAL

I attach a copy of a letter rec from a Mr C N_____. As you can see, he is not satisfied with the level of service he is rec from his currant bankers. I am delighted that he chose to write to us requesting details of our services. A copy of my reply are also attached. // This is not the first customer (1) who has ~~chosen~~ decided to transfer there bus to us. It appears that some of our competitors in the district are losing custome because of poor customer service. Where poss, we should take these opps to increase bus.

A new advertising campaign should be launched. The emphasis should be on our caring attitude towards our customers. Perhaps we could combine this with the wide range of financial services we offer. The campaign could be on the lines of "Everyone is happy at Grange Bank plc." We could show different customers each with a different financial problem. //

Obviously the large-scale advertising campaigns are devised and produced by advertising agents employed by head office. ~~These are very expensive and are for television.~~ However, local branches are able to put together small-scale relevent advertising that meets local needs.

Please put together some ideas for a local campaign. A written proposal must acompany any draught advertisements. The proposal for such an advertising campaign must be submitted to head office before any advertising can be booked. You will also need to find out the costs for advertising in the local newspaper.

I would like to have yr proposal by next Wednesday (insert date) at the latest.

Exam Practice 6 Document 3

WP **T**

Double line-spacing except where indicated.

Banking in the 90s ← Centre this heading

Banking has come a long way from the days when only the rich had bank a/cs. In the passed, banking halls were quiet, formal places. People spoke in hushed tones and speed of service was unheard of.

Customers were treated with the utmost respect. However it was felt that the manager and staff were unapproachable. Women rarely had there own bank a/cs. Generally, a single working woman had to ask a mail relative to gutee her financial affairs before she was allowed to open an a/c.

The services offered by Grange Bank plc have also moved with the times. You can bring all yr financial needs to us. Book an appointment with our specialists. The consultation is free of charge.

Grange Bank plc still treats its customers with respect. Each customer is seen as an individual. Whatever yr needs, whatever yr problem, come and talk to us. We are confident we will be able to provide a solution.

We can provide a wide range of services including:

1 Current a/cs
~~2~~ 5 Deposit a/cs
3 Pension plans
~~4~~ 7 Mortgages
~~5~~ 2 Savings plans
~~6~~ 4 Travel services
~~7~~ 8 Share dealing
~~8~~ 6 Student a/cs

Type this section only in single line-spacing

Current A/c

Customers who keep their a/cs in credit do not pay any ~~charges~~ fees. ①
If you are transfering yr a/c from another bank we ask for a ref. Provided this is satisfactory, we will issue you with a cheque guntee card and cashpoint card straightaway.* If you have not held an a/c before then we will issue a cheque guntee card and cashpoint card after —— months' satisfactory banking.

Once yr a/c has been established, we will agree an overdraft facility with you. This ~~should~~ will give you piece of mind should you have an unexpected exp.

Travel Services

If you are travelling abroad, whether on business or taking the holiday of a lifetime, Grange Bank plc offers many services.

We can help with insurance, traveller's cheques, Eurocard and foreign currency. The commission rates for foreign currency are very competitive. We can supply most currencies without prior notice. Our travellers' insurance policies will ensure piece of mind whilst travelling aboard, however long your stay.

Insert this section (51mm) from left margin

* For customers who have their salary paid into their current a/c, a cheque guntee card of up to £100 can be issued.

Deposit A/cs

For those who require instant access to their money, our deposit a/cs attract an ~~extra high~~ excellent rate of interest. These are sutabb for clubs and society's to use.**

Pension Plans

It is never to early to start planning for your retirement. On average you will need a pension of at least ______________ yr final annual salary. Our pensions adviser will be able to give you the best independent advice available. Should you decide to take out a personnel pension plan, we are confident you will find ours are among the best performers on the market.

Mortgages

Endowment, repayment, pension or PEP, the choice is wide and can be confusing. Our mortgage experts will help you unravel this complicated area. Weather you would like a capped, fixed or variable rate, you will find our mortgages are flexable.

Grange Bank plc does not believe in gimmicks and you won't find us offering large discounts or cashback. However, unlike most other lenders we do not tie you down by making you stay with us for a long period. Large penalties for early redemption are not imposed on our borrowers.

emphasise this sentence

** We also have a special a/c for clubs and Societies. Please ask for further details.

Share Dealing

Grange Bank plc provides a comprehensive sharedealing and portfolio administration service. Our specialists in this area can advise you on the performance of yr shares.

We can give you 24 hours a day access to yr investment portfolio so that you can make an informed decision. Each quarter we will send you a full portfolio valuation so that you can see exactly how yr investments are preforming.

These are just a few of the services we offer, call in at yr local branch to find out more about us. Our staff will be delighted to help.

Word Processing

The Stage III Word Processing Part 2 examination offered by RSA Examinations Board tests your ability to produce a variety of documents from handwritten and typewritten drafts as well as recalled text.

You will be asked to type four documents in one and three quarter hours. These are

1 a multi-page report/article
2 an A4 landscape table with ruling
3 a two-column article or report (newspaper style)
4 a letter or memorandum.

You should ensure that second and subsequent pages of a document are numbered.

In order to pass the examination you must complete the paper within the time given and incur no more than 14 faults. If you incur only 5 faults or less, you will be awarded a distinction.

Three of the tasks in this examination include text that has previously been keyed in by your tutor including saved phrases. The examination requires you to recall two of the previously saved files and make amendments as instructed. One of the documents requires you to recall *part* of a previously saved file. When inserting a paragraph of text, make sure your cursor is placed exactly where you want the paragraph to appear. Do not forget to leave a space before the paragraph is inserted and make sure you insert the correct paragraph. Some of the recalled text includes deliberate errors, which need to be located and corrected, as well as page breaks, which will need to be altered as instructed.

The text which needs to be keyed in for the purpose of the word processing mock examination papers in this book can be found on pages 12–35.

When working on the multi-page document, you should make all the changes regarding line spacing, line length and justification before you start. You also need to ensure that continuation sheets are numbered.

The landscape table must be formatted for wide (landscape) printing as instructed. The ruling may be carried out on the word processor and/or by hand. Make sure you rule the table correctly as each line omitted will incur a fault.

When displaying work in newspaper style, it does not matter if the columns are uneven nor whether they are justified or unjustified.

You should ensure that you use the correct stationery for the letter or memo. Letters must be produced on letterheads and memos on pre-printed forms. Remember to date letters and memos with the date of the examination. If you are asked to take extra copies, make sure you print the required number and indicate the routing on your extra copies.

The letterheads and pre-printed memo form for use with the word processing examination papers which follow can be found on pages 108–113.

A tear-off Resource Sheet will be included at the back of the examination paper from which you will be required to select and extract specific information for inclusion in one or more documents as instructed. The resource sheets for the mock examination papers in this book appear as the last document of each examination paper.

The tasks will contain corrections and amendments for you to make. You will also be asked to move text to different locations in a document and copy text. When moving a paragraph of text, make sure you place the cursor in the correct position and when copying text, make sure the text appears at least twice.

One of the documents will contain lists of information which requires sorting into alphabetical or numerical/chronological order. When sorting the information, make sure each item is included.

When instructed, you must ensure that you have printed a header on each page. If you are asked to change a word or phrase, make sure you change each instance.

When asked to leave a certain amount of space or to insert text by a certain measurement, you must remember to leave the correct amount of space.

Make sure that you have printed all the tasks before handing in your examination work.

One problem candidates face is running out of time in the examination. Not only must you complete the examination paper but also you should have enough time left to check your work carefully. When you are working through the mock examination papers in this section, you may like to make a note of the time each document has taken. As a guide you should aim to complete the tasks within the following time scale.

- Multi-page report/article – 25 minutes
- Landscape table – 30 minutes
- Two-column article – 20 minutes
- Letter or memo – 15 minutes

This will allow you a total of 15 minutes to read the instructions before you type and to check through your work on completion.

Exam Practice 1 Document 1

WP

Recall this document stored under AGENCY1 and amend as shown. Adjust margins to give a line length of 14cm. Change to double line-spacing (except where indicated) and use full justification. Insert and delete page breaks so that the document prints on 4 pages. Save as AGENCY4 and print one copy.

Moving Home ← Change to CAPS please

Moving home is one of lifes most ~~stressful~~ exciting events. Experts rate ~~is~~ it as the third most stressful happening. It is just below the death of a spouce or divorce. [Whilst it is recognised that moving home is difficult, you can take steps to ensure your move goes as smoothly as possible.

underscore this heading

Choosing an Estate Agency

Change the typeface and/or pitch size for this paragraph only.

What to look for

Once you have decided to move, your first step is to register your property with an estate agent. Look in your local news paper or property paper to find some companies. Ask family and friends if they can recomend a reputable agency.

Before you decide check the following:

This section in single line-spacing

1 Does the agency advertise in the local paper regularly?
2 Are the property details they prepare accurate and interesting?
3 Do they take colour photographs of your home?
4 Will your property details be held at each of their branches?
5 Are the staff enthusiastic and motivated?

move this section to point marked ✱

Try to find out what other propery's the agency has sold in your area in recent months. Beware of agents who tell you they can sell your property in a very short period of time.

Page 2 starts here

The Valuation

It is a good idea to ask at least three local companies to value your property. Make sure that they will provide this service free of charge. This should give you a realistic idea of how much your home may fetch. It may not be the best idea to register with the agency ~~who~~ that quotes an very high figure. This may mean your property will take a long time to sell.

✱

Commission

Ask each agency how much commission ~~they~~ it charges. The difference in fees between agencies can mean large savings for you. It is usual for the comission charge to be approximatly 2% - 3% of the puchase price. If you register with just one agent, and

Insert BUYING AND SELLING A PROPERTY as a header and Art. SLS.931.2 as a footer. Header and footer to appear on every page.

agree to keep your property with them for a specified period, they may offer a discount. Registering with 2 or more agencies will add another ½%-1% to their commission charges.

(Page 3 starts here)

Viewings

Generally, estate agencies will not allow you to arrange viewings privately. If you ~~see~~ sell your property through a friend or relative, you will still be liable to pay your agent their commission.

A good agency will be keen to arrange as many viewings as possible. Check that ~~they~~ an agent will accompany prospective purchasers, particularly if you are ~~at~~ in your home alone. Make it clear that you will not receive viewers unless they have previously arranged an appointment.

(Inset this paragraph 25mm from both margins)

(Page 4 starts here)

Property Details

When the agent arrives to measure your property, spend some time with them discusing the best features of your home. Point out any work you have undertaken, particulary central heating, a new roof, re-wiring etc. If yr home has any interesting features these should be stated on the property details.

Ensure that you check the details before they are sent out to prospective purchasers. Ask for details to be changed if you feel they are inaccurate or do not make the best of yr home.

(Copy this sentence to point marked Δ)

By following these guidelines you should be able to choose a reputable agent.

(Change home to house throughout this document)

Exam Practice 1 Document 2

WP

Please key in as shown. Save as AGENCY5 and print one copy with the longest edge at the top. Rule as shown.

Current Potential Purchasers - August

Name	Telephone Number	Requirements	Price £ Thousands
Mr and Mrs Phipps	01289 378292	3 bed period property, garage and garden	80-90
Miss Northedge	01289 379265	1-2 bed flat, Central location	40-50

Refer to the resource sheet to complete all the remaining details from the table. Follow the layout given here.

Properties Registered in August

Property Address	Outline Description	Price £ Thousands
45 Queen Road, Bath	2 bedroom house, small garden	50
32 Edward Avenue, Bath	3 bedroom semi-detached house, garden, double garage	78
91 Waltham Place, Chippenham	4 bedroom, modern detached house, garden, double garage	85
7 Golden Street, Bath	2 bedroom terrace, needs improvement	42
25 Chaucer Lane, Bath	1 bedroom flat in excellent decorative order	45

Exam Practice 1 Document 3

WP

Recall this document stored under AGENCY2 and amend as shown. Display the whole document in 2 columns (newspaper style). Save as AGENCY6 and print one copy.

3

ADVERTISEMENT FEATURE

PHOENIX PROPERTY AGENCY

Phoenix Property Agency has been trading successfully in this area for 21 years. Its distinctive blue and yellow signs are a familiar sight throughout the region. Phoenix signs can be seen ~~promoting~~ Selling flats, houses, bungalows and even manor houses.

Leave a space here, in left column only at least 25mm across by 50mm down, but no more than 30mm across by 60mm down. Do NOT RULE BOX.

The Branch Manager, William Fitzgerald, stated: "Phoenix Property Agency has survived the housing recession because of its caring and professional approach to selling property. We pride ourselves on our high standards of customer care."

Phoenix Property Agency has seventeen branches throughout the region and can be found in local community areas as well as high streets. Many of our branches are attached to a Phoenix Building Society for increased customer convenience.

Buying and selling property can often be fraught with difficulties. The financial help offered by Phoenix Building Society can ~~make~~ go a long way to making this difficult time much easier. Financial Services include mortgages, pensions, PEPS, property and home contents insurance.

Once a property has been registered, a member of staff will visit your property to take measurements. Attractive full-colour property details are prepared and sent to all branches in the region. The details are also added to our extensive database where they will be matched with prospective buyers' requirements. Regular, full-colour advertisements are taken in local newspapers each week.

To take advantage of this marvellous deal, all you need to do is register your property for sale with Phoenix Property Agency during the month of September.

To celebrate 21 years in business, Phoenix Property Agency is offering clients the chance to sell their property for only 1% commission. Of course, the usual 'no sale, no fee' guarantee applies.

Clients know they will receive a first-class service from staff who are motivated to sell their property.

Exam Practice 1 Document 4

WP

Key in as shown and save as AGENCY7
Top + 2 please. One for Paul Williams
and one for file. Indicate routing.

Memo to Matthew Soames from Carole Hill
ref MS/CA/MD

29 LYME AVE ← Centre this heading

This property has been placed with us by (Please insert the names from the resource sheet of the new clients).

It is a semi-detached house with garage and is in excellent decorative order. The property comprises 3 large bedrooms, family bathroom, lounge, dining room, study and luxury Kitchen/breakfast room. The master bedroom has an en-suite shower. The garden is large and contains:

Rockery
Vegetable plot
Lawns
Patio
Greenhouse

(Sort into exact alphabetical order)

The purchase price is to be in the region of £97,000.

The current owners need to sell the property quickly as they have found a house they wish to buy. Please ensure the details are prepared immediately and distributed to all branches in the region.

(Insert the 2nd paragraph of the document stored as AGENCY3)

Property details must also be sent to suitable prospective buyers who are on our mailing database. Please ensure that the buying requirements are carefully matched and checked. This will ensure we do not annoy clients by sending them information on properties that are not suitable for them. // I am pleased we have been asked to deal with the sale of this property as it is outside of our usual area. If we can find a buyer within a couple of weeks, we may be able to secure more business from this part of the city.

Resource Sheet for Exam Practice 1

WP

RESOURCE SHEET

Name	Telephone No	Price £ Thousands	Requirements
Mr & Mrs Phipps	01289 378292	80 - 90	3 bed period property, garage and garden
Miss Northedge	01289 379265	40 - 50	1-2 bed flat, central location
Mr Carter	01684 844126	150 - 200	4 bed semi-detached house, large garden, must have a double garage
Mr Janson	01354 213196	70 - 80	3 bed semi, post 1920, garden
Mr & Mrs Bally	01694 886621	65 - 80	2 bed bungalow, must be on bus route
Ms Kennett	01354 298776	55 - 60	2 bed house, must be in good order
Mr & Mrs Singh	01289 367543	90 - 100	4 bed terrace, must be near Jordan School
Mr & Mrs Murphy	01354 542193	70 - 85	4 bed house, prepared to renovate
Mr Peters	01289 354432	45 - 48	1 bed flat, in good order

Note

Mr and Mrs Dinning have placed 29 Lyme Avenue with us for sale. They would like the purchase price to be in the region of £97,000

Exam Practice 2 **Document 1**

WP

Recall this document stored under HOLIDAY1 and amend as shown. Adjust margins to give a line length of 14cm. Change to double linespacing (except where indicated) and use full justification. Insert and delete page breaks so that the document prints on 4 pages. Save as HOLIDAY4, and print one copy.

Please change places to resorts throughout this document

Holidays are something that everyone looks forward to. This last year has shown an increase in more breaks being taken in this country than for many years.

We need to advertise and attract more people to our holidays both at home and abroad. ← if we are to maintain our profit levels.

Leave space here of at least 35mm from left margin by 50mm down, but no more than 45mm across and 60mm down.

booklets ✓

Our ~~brochures~~ for this season are now available for distribution. The opening page states how our holidays all include full board, free wine with meals, activities, entertainment and excursions. Tourists will require money to cover their own personal expenses and any optional excursions. [Self-catering is an alternative.

Move this sentence to point marked (A)

We have a wide choice of destinations in [Great Britain] Europe and the Mediterranean. The hotels we use range from large ones with plenty of accommodation and organised entertainment to small family-run ones with a somewhat quieter atmosphere. At most places we offer a varied programme of activities. ←

We need to stress the importance of these points when talking to prospective holiday-makers. (Car hire is available.)

Page 2 starts here

(A)

[Self-catering holidays are for those who wish to have a carefree break, where their time will be their own.

Copy this paragraph to point marked (B)

many

We have apartments in a variety of places. Whether one or two bedroom apartments, each will have a separate lounge, kitchen area and ~~separate~~ bathroom. The facilities in each include the following:

Crockery
Cutlery
Cooking utensils
Fridge
Iron and ironing board
Hairdryer
Linen and towels
Maid service
Telephone
Oven and cooking rings

Sort this list into exact alphabetical order

Insert WORLD HOLIDAYS as a header and 1999 SEASON as a footer. Header and footer to appear on every page

Page 3 starts here

(B)

Explain when booking these that linen and towels will be changed each week and that all apartments have heating, gas and electricity. These are included in the price.

This section only in single linespacing

and abroad

Coach tours at home are still very popular. All tours are accompanied by a courier ~~and a driver~~. Our coaches are well upholstered for a comfortable ride. For the additional comfort of passengers, there is no smoking and no loud intrusive music on all coaches. We need to advertise for more couriers for our French tours.

Inset this paragraph 25mm from both left and right margins

New to our itinerary this year is a tour which includes a leisurely cruise for holiday-makers to enjoy. They can discover the classical sites of Greece on a tour combined with a cruise around the Greek Islands.

This is sure to be a very attractive addition to our brochure.

Page 4 starts here

Special interest breaks are always well booked. ~~Some are solidly booked for the next 2 years~~. This year we have added a visit to a banana plantation and botanical garden whilst on our "Gardens in Tenerife" break. [A hiking holiday in the Derbyshire Dales with an experienced guide will allow walkers to experience the peace and tranquility of the Dales.

If any member of your staff can achieve a 10% increase in holidays to places on the Western Isles, ~~they~~ will receive a free 2-day break there for two ~~themselves~~.

Exam Practice 2 Document 2

WP

Please key in as shown. Save as HOLIDAY5 and print one copy with longest edge at the top. Rule as shown.

RESORT HOLIDAYS 1997 ← Centre this heading

Resort	Amenities	Departure Date	Duration (nights)	Price Per Person £
Corfu	Outdoor swimming pool with sun terrace and sunbeds	1 September	7	475
Crete	Games room with snooker tables and table tennis	29 April	7	395

Refer to Resource Sheet to complete all the remaining details of this table. Follow the layout given here.

VERONA OPERA FESTIVAL

Title	Brief Details of Opera	Tour Details
Carmen	Bizet's tragic tale set in Seville	Choose from a 5, 6 or 7-night tour staying in hotels on the shores of Lake Garda. An excursion to Venice can be included.
Madam Butterfly	Puccini's tragic story of a young Japanese girl	
Macbeth	A popular Verdi opera	

Exam Practice 2 Document 3

WP

Recall this document stored under HOLIDAY2 and amend as shown. Display the whole document in 2 columns (newspaper style). SAVE as HOLIDAY6 and print one copy.

BOATING HOLIDAYS FOR ALL AGES

Boating holidays will appeal to all age groups. It is a relaxing and different holiday away from all the everyday cares of life. ~~Everyone has the chance to join in~~.

Discover Britain along the ~~winding rivers~~ stretching waters and canals. Cruise along these picturesque waterways at a gentle pace. Go ashore at your leisure whenever you wish and explore country side villages and historic towns. You will have opportunities to fish, cycle or just walk through beautiful countryside. You can moor alongside waterside inns and restaurants.

Select a holiday from the following parts of the country. [This paragraph only in all capitals]

Kennet and Avon Canal

Miles and miles of idyllic boating through this conservation area. This area of water is lock-free and so you can meander along at a leisurely pace, admiring the wildlife and listening to the birdsong around you. Visit the beautiful city of Norwich with its two cathedrals and a castle.

The Norfolk Broads [Change the typeface and/or pitch size for this paragraph only]

From Bristol to London this canal will take you through rural England and give you an opportunity to experience the industrial heritage of the waterway for yourself.

Stratford-upon-Avon

On the River Avon you can moor opposite the Royal Shakespeare Theatre. Spend time looking around Stratford-upon-Avon before cruising on to Anne Hathaway's Cottage.

Scotland's lochs

Distant mountains and rugged moors will be your scenery as you cruise through the magnificent surroundings along the lochs and canals in Scotland. Autumn is a spectacular time to see the forests in golden and bronze colours.

3

Exam Practice 2 Document 4

WP

Key in as shown and save as HOLIDAY7. Top + 2 please. One for Tour Leader and one for file. Indicate routing.

Our ref RE/Holidays 97

Letter to Mrs Valerie Rogers The Vicarage North Road SPALDING Lincs PE11 2PN

Dear Mrs Rogers

CHRISTMAS HOLIDAY IN HARROGATE

Thank you for your recent letter enquiring about the above holiday. I understand that you would like to make a party booking for 10 people including yourself, subject to space being available. I am delighted to tell you that your party will in fact take the last places available.

Your holiday will include arriving in Harrogate on 23 December and your hotel will be the Old Post House. There will be a welcome sherry reception in the evening followed by a talk on Harrogate.

On Christmas Eve we will have a guided tour of Y_____ Minster. There will be live musical accompaniment during dinner.

Insert here the 2nd paragraph of the document stored as HOLIDAY3.

On 26 December there will be a morning excursion to Ripon Cathedral and onto Fountains Monastery. The afternoon will be free for you to explore Harrogate for yourself.

Check this word and amend if necessary

On the following morning we all make for home after breakfast.

Your tour leader for the break will be (please insert name from Resource Sheet) Peter is a very experienced leader who has led this type of group at Christmas for 3 years now.

We hope you will enjoy your traditional Christmas celebrations in Harrogate. All excursion fees are included in the holiday cost.

Yours Sincerly

Ruth Edwards
Tour Organiser

Resource Sheet for Exam Practice 2

WP

DATABASE FOR RESORT HOLIDAYS 1997

Departure Date	Duration (nights)	Resort	Amenities	Price Per Person £
1 September	7	Corfu	Outdoor swimming pool with sun terrace and sunbeds	475
29 April	7	Crete	Games room with snooker tables and table tennis	395
7 May	14	Rhodes	Poolside bar, gift shop and air conditioning throughout	599
27 May	21	Tenerife	TV room, mini golf	695
7 June	7	Isle of Lewis	Vegetarian diets provided	315
23 December	4	Harrogate	Excursions to York Minster, Ripon Cathedral and Fountains Abbey	295

Note from Ruth to all Leaders.

Please note that the Harrogate Christmas Holiday will be led by Peter Williams again this year. A number of guests are returning this year and have specifically asked for Peter.

3

Exam Practice 3 Document 1

WP

Recall this document stored under AUCTION1 and amend as shown. Adjust margins to give a line length of 12cm. Change to double line-spacing (except where indicated) and use full justification. Insert and delete page breaks so that the document prints on 4 pages. Save as AUCTION4 and print one copy.

Auctions

Buying at an auction is great fun. You can pick up some incredible bargains. However, you must follow a few simple rules or you may end up with more than you antcipated.

(✓) To ~~find out~~ discover where the auction rooms are, look in your local news paper or phone book. Usually sales are held every month. ~~Most towns will have at least one auction room~~. General household sales are the most common. These sell everything from furniture to bric a brac. Specialist sales are held less frequently, in these you will find fine art, silver, jewellery, antiques etc.

This paragraph only in single line-spacing

Move this paragraph to point marked (A)

Purchasing a property through auction can often mean acquiring a property at a very realistic price. However, it can also be a gamble. The same rules apply to property's as any other goods sold through auction. Once the hammer drops you are legally obliged to complete the purchase.

A catalogue is usually produced for each sale. These can cost from £1 to £15 or £20 for a full colour specialist catalogue. It is worth investing in a catalogue a few days before the sale so that you can study it at your liesure.

Viewings are held a day or two before the auction and on the day itself. It is a good idea to go along and see what is on offer. If you are planning to purchase an item, check it carefully for damage or wear and tear. Remember, once you have successfully bid for an item you have a legal obligation to purchase it.

Page 2 starts here

On the day of the sale, try to arrive a little early. ~~Check the items again and~~ Have another look at the items you wish to purchase. decide on a price that you are willing to pay for each item.

Whatever you do, do not get carried away with the excitment of the sale and bid in excess of your reserve price.

Copy this paragraph to point marked (B).

Change the typeface/pitch size for this paragraph only

When the bidding commences check that you can hear the auctioneer clearly. Before you enter the bidding ensure you are competing for the correct article. This sounds obvious, but you may find you end up purchasing a completley unsuitable item because you confused the catalogue numbers.

(B)

If you are fortunate enough to make a successfull bid you will be expected to pay a deposit for your goods. This may be approximately 10% of the bid price.

Page 3 starts here

The full purchase price and commission fee must be paid within a specified period. This is usually 3 days. The goods must be collected straightaway or you may be liable for storage fees.

(A)

This means that if you require a mortgage this must be arranged before the auction date. Discuss this with your building society manager or other mortgage lender well in advance of the auction. You will have to pay for a surveyors report and any mortgage arrangement fees in advance. A solicitor must also be appointed to carry out the Land Registry and local searches before the bidding commences.

Page 4 starts here

This does mean you may incurr expenses of around £500 - £1000 and lose the purchase to another party. However, if you are successful, you must be able to pay the 10% deposit before leaving the auction rooms. // You will have the satisfaction of knowing that you have purchased your home at a realistic price.

Happy bargain hunting and good luck!

A commission fee will also be levied.

Inset this paragraph 25 mm from each margin

Insert a header Information Sheet and a footer SLS.3.2.9.7. Header and footer to appear on every page.

Exam Practice 3 Document 2

WP

Please key in as shown. Save as AUCTIONS and print one copy with the longest edge at the top. Rule as shown.

Auction – October

Vendor	Item	Reserve Price	Catalogue No	Estimated Price
Mr Peter Jones	Clarice Cliff Teapot	£850.00	CB650	£1000 – £2000
Mrs Kathy Howell	Steiff Teddy Bear	£300.00	TB411	£500 – £600
Ms Jenny Wood	Georgian Sewing Box	£750.00	MB699	£800 – £1000

Refer to the resource sheet to complete all the remaining details from the table. Follow the layout given here.

Items to be valued for December Sale		
Item	Vendor	Notes
18th-century musical box	Raymond Withy	In fair condition, vendor says he has repaired it himself.
17th-century laquered box	Doreen Metcalfe	Good condition.
Diamond and Sapphire necklace	Vincent Bembridge	The clasp needs attention. The Jewels are set in 18 carat gold.
Susie Cooper Dinner Service	Eleanor Grant.	This was found in the attic. It is in excellent condition.
18th-century Chaise longue	Helen Berry	Needs re-upholstering, some damage to frame.

Exam Practice 3 Document 3

WP

Recall this document stored under AUCTION2 and amend as shown. Display the whole document in 2 columns (newspaper style). Save as AUCTION6 and print one copy.

3

October Sale

Household and General Items

Leave a space here of at least 20mm across by 35mm down, but no more than 25mm across by 45mm down. Left column only. Do NOT RULE BOX.

The October sale will be held at 10 am on the first Monday of the month. Viewing will take place on the Friday and Saturday prior to the sale. The viewing times are 10.30 am - 6.00 pm Friday, 10.00 am - 2.00 pm Saturday. Catalogues are available at a cost of ← Insert this detail from the Resource Sheet.

These monthly sales are always well-attended as local people realise they can pick up bargains for their homes. It is advisable to arrive promptly as the saleroom is often packed to capacity.

This month, items on sale include:

Pine dressers
Sideboards
Wardrobes
Dining room table
Sofas
Washing machine
Kitchen table
Writing bureau
Dining room chairs
Piano

← Sort into exact alphabetical order

The reserve price of some of the items is very low. We guarantee that there will be plenty of bargains to be found.

If you cannot attend the sale in person you can still make a bid for any of the items on sale. Leave your bid and telephone number with a member of our competent staff. ← They will bid on your behalf and advise you of the outcome.

Please remember, if you are successful in your bid you must be prepared to pay for and collect your purchases within 48 hours of the sale. Failure to do so will incur storage charges.

As well as the household and general items' sales we also have regular specialist auctions. These include ceramics, fine art, tapestry, special collections and silver. Details of all these events are published in the specialist magazines and local newspaper.

If you would like to be informed in advance of these specialist auctions then we would be delighted to do so. Write or telephone and give details of your name and address. ← State which sales you are interested in. We will ensure you receive advance notification of all our events.

Exam Practice 3 Document 4

WP

Key in as shown and save as AUCTION7.
Top + 2 please. One for Geoffrey Ferguson and 1 for file.
Indicate routing.

Memo to Tristan Charlton from Miranda Alyson
Ref NYS/1/992.6.3

Next Year's Sales ← Change to CAPS

It really is time we planned next year's sales. I know that however well we organise the auctions our calendar is re-arranged many times, but we do need a draft outline.

Perhaps we could meet soon to discuss this in greater detail. If possible, Wednesday of next week would be convenient. I am available all day. Let my Secretary know what time would be suitable for you.

I thought the best place to start would be to look at the previous few years. It may be that we should be much more analytical when organising the sales. For example, it occurred to me that it makes sense to hold sales of expensive items in November and December when customers are willing to spend. January and February are terrible months to hold auctions of fine art.

On a completely different topic, we need to appoint an auctioneer as Martin leaves the company next month. I have been searching through the computer files and found this personal quality description. I feel we could use this in the advertisement. Perhaps you would let me have your thoughts.

Insert the first paragraph of the document stored as AUCTION3

The advertisement should appear in the specialist magazines next month. If you agree to the draft then my secretary will book the advertisements straightaway. I hope we will be able to find an auctioneer as talented as Martin.

Resource Sheet for Exam Practice 3

WP

RESOURCE SHEET

Item	Vendor	Reserve Price	Cat No	Estimated Price
Clarice Cliff Teapot	Mr Peter Jones	£850.00	CB650	£1000 - £2000
Steiff Teddy Bear	Mrs Kathy Howell	£300.00	TB411	£500 - £600
Georgian Sewing Box	Ms Jenny Wood	£750.00	MB699	£800 - £1000
Victorian Pine Dresser	Mrs Mary Brind	£890	HB111	£900 - £1200
Silver Candelabra	Mr Adam More	£1000	MB694	£1000 - £1200
Porcelain Figurine	Mr Roger Evans	£380	CB590	£300 - £450
Bakelite Radio	Ms Hannah Felts	£200	MB621	£150 - £250
Oak Sideboard	Mr James Saks	£1300	HB192	£1100 - £1300
Yew Dining Table	Ms Chloe Reese	£1500	HB184	£1500 - £2500

Note

The print costs for the sale catalogue have increased. We shall have to charge £2.50 per catalogue to cover these costs.

Exam Practice 4 Document 1

WP

Recall this document stored under NEWHOME1 and amend as shown. Adjust margins to give a line length of 14cm. Change to double linespacing (except where indicated) and use full justification. Insert and delete page breaks so that the document prints on 4 pages. Save as NEWHOME2 and print one copy.

Please change property to housing throughout this document

Move this section to point marked (A)

Confidence started to return to the market in earnest last autumn. Fears of an interest rate rise to control inflationary pressures on the economy appear to have passed by. With spring just around the corner and confidence continuing in the property market, we need more new properties on our ~~books~~ ledgers. Page 2 starts here

There is nothing ~~It would appear that nothing~~ that can now dampen the property market resurgence.

For months there has been an increase in the percentage of survey contributions reporting price increases with the number of sales also increasing. There is a 20% increase in the number of sales compared with last year.

Copy this paragraph to point marked (B)

Improved market conditions, together with realistic pricing has encouraged more activity in the property market.

(A)

The following is a list of areas ~~Some areas are listed~~ where we still have large properties forsale.

Sort this list into exact alphabetical order

Claverton Down
Entry Hill Gardens
Abingdon Terrace
Fairfield Park
New King Street
Moorfields Road
Royal Crescent
St Catherine's Valley
The Ley
Park Street

(B)

Insert MONTHLY BULLETIN as a header and MARCH 1997 as a footer. Header and footer to appear on every page.

The Ley area has a substantial 4-bedroom traditional farmhouse for sale. It has 3 reception rooms and oil central heating. Situated in an unspoilt rural position. A superb family home.

Leave a space here of at least 25mm from right margin by 35mm down but no more than 35mm across and 50mm down

An immaculate 4-bedroom semi-detached house situated in St Catherine's Valley offers a lounge, dining hall, fitted kitchen, bathroom, separate shower room and a pleasant garden. It is in the vicinity of the village and a few minutes ' walk away from fields and open countryside. ~~The perfect setting to live~~.

Page 3 starts here

We now need to run a special promotion [on these houses] whilst the market is so buoyant. John Atkins will be responsible for this and he will let you have the details within the next week. Good quality, attractive literature will encourage potential buyers.

New [housing] developments continue to expand in our location. Prices range from around £40,000 to £250,000 with an average price of £60,000 for a 3-bedroom semi-detached home. ~~There is a shortage of bungalows~~.

Change this paragraph to single linespacing and inset it 25mm from both left and right margins

Houses at the lower end of the market are priced between £44,000 and £48,500. Depending on the location, the 2-bedroomed version, complete with parking space, would include kitchen~~s~~ with fitted oven and hob.

Most of these developments are within easy travelling distance of Bath and Bristol. Keep an attractive display of these developments in your showroom and have up-to-date information readily available.

All branches should participate in the promotion and be active in the marketing side using regular advertising.

These are ideal for the first-time buyer market and are selling quickly.

Page 4 starts here

Since our meeting last month it is apparent that a more professional approach has been made to the residential lettings and management side of our business. Demand for good quality properties continues and I am sure we can be optimistic for the future.

This section only in all capitals

Exam Practice 4 Document 2

WP

Please key in as shown. Save as NEWHOMES and print one copy with longest edge at the top. Rule as shown.

NEW HOMES IN THE SOUTH WEST (Centre this heading)

Name	Address	Property Type	Completion Date	Price £
Knighton Court	Lush Valley, Barnstaple	4-bedroom houses	June 1997	150,000
Vale View	Cathedral Close, Truro	2-bedroom bungalows	October 1997	91, 950

Refer to the Resource Sheet to complete all the remaining details of this table. Follow the layout given here.

SHOW HOME DETAILS FOR CORNWALL

Selling Agents	Development	Fixtures and Accessories
Jones and Watson Edwards Property Services Vincent and Broad Group	Beacon View, St Agnes The Thornbury, Marazion Timber Touch, Truro	All show houses will be sold with fitted carpets and curtains. Fixtures include fitted wardrobes in master bedroom. Table lamps and other ancillary items can be purchased at a discount price.

Exam Practice 4 Document 3

WP

Recall this document stored under NEWHOME2 and amend as shown. Display the whole document in 2 columns (newspaper style). Save as NEWHOME6 and print one copy.

A VIEW OF ST AGNES, CORNWALL

Jones and Watson are pleased to give this brief outline of the area in which Beacon View has been developed.

Local amenities include a good library, post office, two banks and a doctor's surgery. The shops in the village cater for daily provisions, clothes and footwear, pharmaceuticals, gifts and sundries. There is a frequent bus service into Truro which has an excellent shopping centre.

Landscape

In the 18th and 19th centuries this was the bustling centre of a flourishing mining area. Although the majority of the mining was for tin, some copper mining also took place. St Agnes lies on a hillside and the surrounding landscape is dotted with old mine workings, tall chimneys and engine-houses.

History

~~Slate and granite cottages line the main street~~. The coastline around St Agnes combines the freedom of the clifftops, with a lush agricultural interior. Four steep sided valleys cut into the coastline from the sea. Each valley becomes progressively more wooded as you go inland.

St Agnes Beacon

The Beacon is like ~~a great island~~ ~~huge mound~~ of sedimentary rock standing above the granite. Paths flanked by gorse and heather lead to the summit, which is over 600 feet above sea level. A view from here gives a 30-mile panoramic sweep of the Atlantic coast.

Recreational features include a nearby golf course, horse riding, clay pigeon shooting and tennis. There are also two playing fields, one with a football pitch plus play equipment.

Village life can be fun. You will be able to take an active part in some of the Annual Events, namely the May Ball or Carnival Week in August.

Change the typeface and/or pitch size for this paragraph only

Exam Practice 4 Document 4

WP

key in as shown and save as NEWHOME7
Top + 2 please. One for Rebecca Morris and one for file. Indicate routing.

Memo to Clare Young from John Atkins
ref HB/PL/1997

SPRING SPECIAL PROMOTION

At the March monthly meeting I was asked to co-ordinate a special promotion for selling some of the larger properties we still have on our books. I would like you to prepare your branch's information for me. Refer any queries you may have to my Secretary, Rebecca Morris.

Please include the following points in your reply.

1 How long the property has been on your books and how many potential buyers have viewed it in the last two months.

2 The asking price and whether you think this is realistic. If the price has been dropped since the original one was fixed, let me know if you think it feasible to lower it again.

3 Insert here the 3rd paragraph of the document stored as NEWHOME3

4 What amenities are in the area for children. You should include schools in this section too. Larger properties are usually bought as family homes and we need to make this a high priority selling point. (Check this word and amend if necessary)

I would like to see the house in St Catherine's Way sold as little interest has apparently been shown in it over the last year.

New photographs of the properties will be taken by (Please insert name from Resource Sheet) and when I have the above information from all branches in the South West, I will endeavour to publish an attractive fact sheet for distribution.

Resource Sheet for Exam Practice 4

WP

DATABASE OF NEW HOMES IN THE SOUTH WEST

Property Type	Price £	Completion Date	Name	Address
4-bedroom houses	150,000	June 1997	Knighton Court	Lush Valley, Barnstaple
2-bedroom bungalows	91,950	October 1997	Vale View	Cathedral Close, Truro
Cottage style homes	72,999	March 1998	Silver Meadows	Silver Street, Devizes
3-bedroom houses	110,550	September 1997	The Hedgerows	North Road, Salisbury
Courtyard apartments	98,999	June 1998	Oak Court	Moat View, Wells
Community style 1-bedroom cottages	31,500	August 1997	Park Place	Cheddar View, Bristol

Note to Rebecca from John

Please remind me to let all branches know we are now using Homes in Camera for all special promotions. They are based in Bristol and have a team of 12 photographers.

<u>Exam Practice 5</u> Document 1

WP

Recall this document stored as GOVERN1. Amend as shown. Adjust margins to give a line length of 14cm. Change to double line-spacing (except where indicated) and use full justification. Insert and delete page breaks so that the document prints on 4 pages. Save as GOVERN4 and print one copy.

School Governing Board

The governing board of each local education authority maintained school is made up of a number of representatives from the school, parents and the local community.

(A)

1 Establishe the aims and policy's of the school and how the required educational standards can be met

2 Deciding how the school should be run

3 Assisting the staff to draw up the school development plan

4 Deciding how to spend the school budget in the most efficient way

5 Ensuring the National Curriculum and religious education are taught

6 Appointing a head teacher

7 Appointing, prommoting, supporting and disciplining other staff

8 Acting as a link between the school and the local community

9 Drawing up an action plan and monitoring its progress

This section only in single line-spacing.

Page 2 starts here

<u>Becoming a School Governor</u>

Each school needs enthusiastic, motivated people who are intrested in the education of young ~~children~~ people. There are a number of parent governors on the governing board of each school.

When a vacancy arises, you can put yourself forward for election. Two parents of ~~the~~ children at the school must support your application. If more than one parent wishes to become a governor, an election will be held. Usually, you can write a short paragraph about yourself and your suitability to hold office. Parents are then asked to vote. ~~The whole process should take no more than three weeks~~.

(B)

Page 3 starts here

What Qualifications Do I Need?

Formal qualifications are not necessary, nor do you need to have any specialist knowledge of education. You will still be able to make a valid contribution to the running of a school. The head teacher and staff will be able to advice you on matters concerning education. You may be able to use your own areas of expertise in helping the school make important decisions.

What you do need is enthusiasm. It helps if you are a good listener. You will then be able to collect many different views on school issues. This will enable you to make informed decisions.

, loyalty and some spare time

Inset this paragraph 2.5cm from both margins

Team working is another important skill. The governing board must work well together and have the schools' best interests at heart. Although the governing board has many duties and responsibilities no individual governor has any powers within the school.

Page 4 starts here

How much time is involved?

The full governing board usually meets at least twice a term. However, Committees dealing with specialised areas such as:

finance
premises
curriculum
personnel
lettings
school development
marketing

Sort into exact alphabetical order

are formed and you may be expected to sit on one or two of these.

As well as attending meetings you may have to read reports and Government papers and visit the school from time to time. This may not take as much time as it first appears. You do however need to make a committment to the school and be prepared to attend meetings regularly.

Move this paragraph to point marked (A)

(J)

The board has a number of ~~duties~~ powers as well as legal responsibilities. The main duties are listed below.

Change typeface and/or pitch/size for this section

For only a few hours each week, you can make a big contribution to the running of your childs school, and help your local community.

Copy this paragraph to point marked (B)

Insert GOVERNING BODY as a header and Information Sheet 3 as a footer. Header and footer to appear on every page.

Change Board to body throughout this document

Exam Practice 5 Document 2

WP

Please key in as shown. Save as GOVERNS and print one copy with the longest edge at the top. Rule as shown.

Parker Primary School – Governing Body

Name	Address	Type of Governor	Start date	Finish date
Mrs S Davison	10 Bath Street, LEEDS LS1 6BY	Parent	10.2.97	10.2.2001
Mrs P Allen	20 Burnham Road, LEEDS LS2 4HK	Co-opted	24.6.95	24.6.99
Mr K Morrison	71 Mount Road, LEEDS LS8 7SL	Teacher	1.11.94	1.11.98

Refer to the resource sheet to complete all the remaining details from the table. Follow the layout given here.

Committee Members

Committee	Responsibilities	Chairperson
Curriculum	To oversee the delivery of the National Curriculum. To ensure that a scheme of work and related resources are up to date and readily available.	Mr K Morrison
Premises	To oversee the maintenance of the school environment. To advise on safety. To advise on lettings policy.	Revd D Vincent
Personnel	To appoint, support, promote staff including head teacher. To follow disciplinary procedures where necessary.	Mrs P Allen
Finance	To manage school budget and advise where necessary.	Dr S Hansome

Exam Practice 5 Document 3

WP

Recall this document stored under GOVERN2 and amend as shown. Display the whole document in 2 columns (newspaper style). Save as GOVERN6 and print one copy.

3

Clerk to the Governors

Parker Primary School is looking ~~for~~ to appoint a new clerk to the governing body. The position would suit someone with school-age children as all committee meetings are held in the evenings. Parker Primary School would ~~particularly~~ especially welcome applications from parents at the school.

As well as secretarial skills, the applicant must be enthusiastic, loyal and above all, discreet. As clerk to the governing body, the post-holder will have access to a great deal of confidential information.

Leave a space here, in left column only at least 20mm across and 60mm down, but no more than 30mm across and 70mm down. Do NOT RULE.

The most suitable candidate will have secretarial skills especially in word processing and general presentation of documents. Shorthand speed would be advantageous as minuting meetings will be the main duty.

The duties will include attending and minuting meetings which will involve approximately six evenings per academic term. Preparing agendas and notices, typing up minutes and distributing to the governing body will also be part of these duties.

Governors' newsletters which go out to parents each term are produced and designed by the clerk. Desktop publishing skills would be an advantage.

The post-holder will also be required to deal with the routine correspondence of the governors. It is anticipated that this should not take longer than 2-3 hours per week. Liaising with the local education authority's link governor committee will also form part of this post.

Training is given and the clerk will have the opportunity to attend courses organised by the local education authority.

An honorarium of approximately £1500 - £2000 will be paid each academic year. ~~This is based on the post-holder working a maximum of 4 hours per week, term-time only.~~ This is reviewed each academic year.

If you are interested in holding this very challenging position, please contact Gerry Miles, the head teacher.

Exam Practice 5 Document 4

WP

Key in as shown and save as GOVERN7. Top + 2 please one copy for Chair of Governors and one for file. Indicate routing. Use headed paper.

Letter to Mrs S Davison, 10 Bath Street, LEEDS LS1 6BY
Our ref LK/SD/431.6

Dear Mrs Davison

Parent Governor Election ← Centre this heading

As returning officer I am pleased to inform you that you have been successful in the above election for parent governor. I am sure you will find the experience both interesting and enjoyable.

The Governing Body of Parker Primary School consists of [Insert number from Resource Sheet] members. This number is dictated by the number of pupils registered. The governors are made up from a variety of people, as set out in Government guidelines.

[Insert paragraphs 2 and 3 from the document stored as GOVERN3 here.]

The Governing Body is divided into four committees: these are premises, finance, personnel and curriculum. They meet on a regular basis, approximately 3 times each term. Reports are made from each committee to the full Governing Body, which meets at least twice each term.

The next meeting of the Governing Body is on the 28th of next month. I look forward to seeing you then.

However, if you would like to discuss your new role further, please contact me.

I am enclosing some information on the School Governing Body which I hope you will find interesting and useful.

Yrs sncly
Gerry Miles
Head teacher

Resource Sheet for Exam Practice 5

WP

Start Date	Name	Type of Governor	Address	Finish Date
10.02.97	Mrs S Davison	Parent	10 Bath Street, LEEDS LS1 6BY	10.02.01
24.06.95	Mrs P Allen	Co-opted	20 Burnham Road, LEEDS LS2 4HK	24.06.99
01.11.94	Mr K Morrison	Teacher	71 Mount Road, LEEDS LS8 7SL	01.11.98
23.09.94	Mrs B Smedley	LEA	3 Magdalen Avenue, LEEDS LS1 4NE	23.09.98
16.04.96	Ms H Lawson	LEA	92 Lillie Road, LEEDS LS1 7TC	16.04.00
05.10.95	Mr L Norwood	LEA	16 Coromandel Heights, LEEDS LS1 8IL	05.10.99
17.01.96	Revd D Vincent	Parent	The Rectory, Ball Street, LEEDS LS1 3WP	17.01.00
30.10.94	Dr S Hansome	Co-opted	30 Audley Park, LEEDS LS2 7GJ	30.10.98
28.03.96	Mrs K Booth	Parent	3 Rosslyn Way LEEDS LS7 6AP	28.03.00
05.05.95	Mr N Ramsey	Co-opted	1 Bellotts Road, LEEDS LS1 9QX	05.05.99
12.09.96	Mrs P Mulligan	Parent	72 Coronation Avenue, LEEDS LS1 8KJ	12.09.00
06.09.94	Mr G Miles	Head	34 Newbridge Hill, LEEDS LS1 2BU	06.09.98

Note

Schools of 100 – 299 pupils may have up to 12 governors

4 parents
3 LEA
4 Co-opted
1 Head teacher

<u>Exam Practice 6</u> Document 1

WP

Recall this document stored under HOBBIES1 and amend as shown. Adjust margins to give a line length of 13cm. Change to double linespacing (except where indicated) and use full justification. Insert and delete page breaks so that the document prints on 4 pages. Save as HOBBIES4 and print one copy.

Change unit to course throughout this document

Move this paragraph to point marked (A)

Whether

Art, painting, sketching or calligraphy, is a wonderful way to relax. We have the unit to suit your individual need and you will find them all described in our part-time programme for this current academic year.

The pace of life today is very stressful. It is very important to use free time sensibly and follow a hobby that will give the mind and body complete relaxation.

(A)

be interested in

weekend

You may ~~have heard of~~ our new workshop on handling conflict with creativity. Relationships at work can be damaged by conflict. This workshop uses art, visualisation and role play to identify needs and communicate feelings of anger or hurt.

in the home or

Page 2 starts here

designed

The unit is ~~suitable~~ for people who are interested in personal growth and it requires no previous art skills. You will need to bring with you:

Cartridge paper
Adhesive tape
Collage materials
Clipboard
Crayons
Pens
Pencils
Scissors
Sketch pad

Sort this list into <u>exact</u> alphabetical order

Change this paragraph to single linespacing and inset it 25mm from both left and right margins.

Many people have an urge to produce water-colours. They do not realise that a good background in the knowledge of drawing is imperative for final success. Many prospective students are impatient and fail to understand the need for discipline and the importance of drawing skills. ~~Patience is a necessary skill for art work~~ Remember, you need confidence to be able to draw. ~~Many people do not realise this~~. copy this paragraph to point marked (B)

Page 3 starts here

If you are a beginner you can join a group and be shown how to draw a variety of objects, also simple perspective.

Progression will take place onto the opportunity of drawing the human form as well as proportion. The group usually consists of people of all ages and abilities. Portraiture will be included in this unit.

If you have already acquired ~~Having established~~ the expertise necessary in drawing forms, you may wish to portray your drawing in terms of water-colour.

The more practice you have had with your pencil, the more freely you will be able to express yourself with the brush.

There are a number of courses for you to choose from. We have a structured course on colour theory and techniques of water-colour. Our syllabus allows for flexibility and does not include methodically prescribed exercises. ~~This can be very boring and uninteresting~~. Room must always be left for self expression.

This section only in all capitals

Page 4 starts here

After attending our courses you will have the background knowledge necessary for you to participate further on your own in your chosen art area. If you wish to enter for a qualification, a GCSE or A-level course will be your next move.

As soon as an idea for a painting is formalised in your mind, set it down in sketch form. Spontaneous paintings are often the result of this ~~outcome of an elaborate~~ form of work.

(B)

Insert RELAXING HOBBIES as a header and ART COURSES as a footer. Header and footer to appear on every page.

3

Exam Practice 6 Document 2

WP

Please key in as shown. Save as HOBBIES5 and print one copy with longest edge at the top. Rule as shown.

CREATIVITY COURSES ← Centre this heading

Title	Leader	Course Code	Fee Code	Course Duration	Commencement Date
Art-Painting Flowers	Mary Jackson	B011/03	JJ	18 weeks	15 September
Life Drawing	John Watson	B003/05	KK	20 weeks	17 September

Refer to the Resource Sheet to complete all the remaining details of this table. Follow the layout given here.

WEEKEND COURSES

Subject	Description	Where	When
Bead Work	How to use beads in embroidery, patchwork and quilting.	Main College	14 and 15 June
Stained Glass	Use traditional glass and lead methods to design and make a small glass panel.	West Hall Church	12 and 13 July
Book Covers	Cover a special book using either plain or patterned fabric.	College Annexe	2 and 3 August

Exam Practice 6 Document 3

WP

Recall this document stored under HOBBIES2 and amend as shown. Display the whole document in 2 columns (newspaper style). Save as HOBBIES6 and print one copy.

CALLIGRAPHY FOR ALL

From an introduction to the foundation hand and capitals to italic style and colour calligraphy, this is a hobby everyone can enjoy. Most courses are for a 10-week block and include the following themes.

Borders with Flowers

Leave a space here, in the left column only, at least 35mm across from left margin by 50mm down, but no more than 45mm across or 60mm down.

Alphabets that will ~~inspire everyone~~ encourage all to design and decorate capital letters. Each alphabet ~~is illustrated and~~ will have basic design instructions together with ideas for variations. Whether you are interpreting the words of a text or perhaps decorating a name, your finished piece of work should be harmonious and pleasing to the eye.

Illuminated Alphabets

Artists have used plants as a source of inspiration for centuries. Delicate flower heads, stems and leaves can be safely entwined round any awkward gap or corner. Flowers can be adapted in a variety of ways. You can use a free-flowing pattern which can be lengthened or shortened as necessary. For a rose border you can decorate the initial letter, paint the inside roses in a water-colour and the bordering branches in gouache.

Colour Style

Although some traditional approaches demand the use of black ink, who can resist colour?

Colour makes calligraphy attractive, more effective and memorable.

Change the typeface and/or pitch size for this paragraph only

A suitable work surface and a comfortable working position are essential for calligraphy and illumination. Use a slanting work surface. A good comfortable chair that is the right height for you will help to prevent backache.

A good quality cartridge paper is ideal for beginners. A set of pencils from the H range and quill, reed and metal-nibbed pens are all essential.

Exam Practice 6 Document 4

WP

Key in as shown and save as HOBBIES7. Top + 2 please. One for Joanne Chambers and one for file. Indicate routing.

Our ref BW/587

Letter to Mrs Dorothy Reed Park View House 31 North Road WAKEFIELD WF1 4HL

Dear Mrs Reed

CREATIVE STUDIES - STAINED GLASS WEEKEND

Thank you for your letter of enquiry concerning the above course. I am pleased to confirm the weekend will be led by Joanne Chambers and will take place in East Hall Church.

Check this word and amend if necessary

You will have the whole weekend in which to design and make your own small stained glass panel. Traditional glass methods will be used and no previous experience is necessary.

Insert here the 2nd paragraph of the document stored as HOBBIES3.

Would you please pay the full amount of £60 at the time of your application. We accept payment by credit card, cash or cheque. Cheques should be made payable to the college with your name and address on the back.

You may enrol in person or by post. The college reception office is open from 9am to Please insert time from Resource Sheet on Monday to Friday. Complete the booking form at the back of your prospectus if you would like to enrol by post.

If you wish to book a place by telephone you will need to have your credit card details, course code and title etc. We will also accept bookings by fax provided you have given your credit card details and authorisation.

Yours Sincerely

Barbara Watson
Course Co-ordinator

Resource Sheet for Exam Practice 6

WP

DATABASE FOR CREATIVITY COURSES

Commencement Date	Course Code	Fee Code	Title	Leader	Course Duration
15 September	B011/03	JJ	Art - Painting Flowers	Mary Jackson	18 weeks
17 September	B003/05	KK	Life Drawing	John Watson	20 weeks
6 October	C015/04	AB	Calligraphy - Beginners	Mavis Stanton	10 weeks
7 October	C002/10	AC	Cloth Sculpture	Anne Hall	12 weeks
10 November	C009/01	AD	Embroidered Boxes	Susan Netherby	6 weeks
18 September	C007/07	AE	Dressmaking	Karen Field	20 weeks

Note to Course Co-ordinator
from Reception Office.

As from 1 January this year we will be closing at 4 pm instead of 5 pm as previously notified.

Letterheads and memo form for photocopying

The letterheads and memo which follow are for use throughout this book and may be photocopied. As there are two letterheads shown on one page, ensure that you cover up the letterhead not needed with a blank sheet of paper when photocopying.

MODERN COMPUTING

Silicone Way
Cribbs Causeway
BRISTOL
BS8 9PU

MEMORANDUM

To

From

Ref

Date

THE TOY
CHEST

Head Office
63 Newall Road
HARROGATE
York
YO1 2NE

Homecare Supplies

Homecare House
Wells Road
READING
RG1 3XW

Somerset Local Authority

Town Hall
SHEPTON MALLET
Somerset
SH8 0NE

Home Design 2000

Unit 4
Park Nurseries Estate
BATH
BA2 4JH

Grange Bank Plc

1 High Street

HASTINGS

E Sussex

HT1 6YV

International House Portman Square LEEDS LS5 1XX

Worldwide Tours

Minster College of Art

Knaresborough Road
YORK
YO2 9BW

Parker
Primary
School

Kingston Avenue
LEEDS
LS40 3QL

Key to proof reading exercises

Proof Reading Practice Exercise 1

WP **T**

MEMORANDUM

To June Grove

From Richard Thomas

Ref RT/AJ

Date (Date of typing)

As term will come to an end next Friday and we begin the summer break, please
1 insure every child in the school takes home a holiday tips sheet. In connection with
older children who can be left alone at home, looking at the sheet we used last year, it
needs to be updated in a number of places.

The paragraph about hot drinks needs redrafting. Include in it teaching children to use
2 mugs and not cups as mugs our less likely to spill. They should only put as much
3 water as they need into a kettle so that it is lightr and easier to pour. It is better to
leave them a hot drink in a thermos if possible.

If they need to make a snack or meal try to leave them something cold, like
sandwiches, or food that can be heated up in a microwave. Buy oven chips to avoid
4 5 the use of a chippan. Use an electric Lighter for the gas to save having to use
matches. Ensure children know how to use any gadget or tools they may have to use
in the kitchen.

6 Before completing the sheet, check what holiday schems will be running in the area.
7 8 Children usually enjoy the facilities they provide and our happier their than at home
9 on there own.

■ Errors

1 The word ensure has been typed incorrectly.

2 The word our has been used instead of are.

3 The word lighter has been spelt incorrectly.

4 The word chip pan has a space missing.

5 A capital letter appears incorrectly at the beginning of a word.

6 The word schemes has been spelt incorrectly.

7 The word our has been used instead of are.

8 The word their has been used instead of there.

9 The word there has been used instead of their.

Proof Reading Practice Exercise 2

WP T

MEMORANDUM

To	Paul Masterson
From	Emma Jones
Ref	PM/Lunch97
Date	(Date of typing)

1 june sales meeting lunch

As we shall have a number of special guests looking round our factory at the time of
2 our June Sales Meeting, I thought we would take them out tolunch.

3 we have been sent a choice of Business Lunch Menus and have decided to choose the
4 following, being Menu B at pounds 12.50 per head. A starter comprising mixed Hors
5 Doeuvres followed by Aromatic Crispy Duck, Sizzling Lamb with Ginger and Spring Onions. Lemon Chicken will follow served with Stir Fried Mixed Vegetables.

6 I have been to the Peking Restaurant in King Street on a number of ocassions and the
7 food has always been exellent. I have booked a table for 15 at 12 noon and hope this will be convenient for you. Please let me know by the end of next week so that I can
8 confirm th3 numbers.

9 I do not think we have any vegatarians on the staff but I would be grateful if you
10 would check on this for me and also the visitors when they arrive. I would mentioned
11 that the Stir Fried Mixed Vegetables are almost a meal on their own? The ingredients include broccoli spears, courgettes, carrots, button mushrooms and fresh beansprouts.

We can look at the wine list when we are there.

12 cc

■ Errors

1 Failure to show heading in initial capitals.

2 The space between to and lunch has been omitted.

3 Capital letter at the beginning of a sentence has been omitted.

4 Inconsistent use of words and figures.

5 D'oeuvres has been spelt incorrectly.

6 Occasions has been spelt incorrectly.

7 Excellent has been spelt incorrectly.

8 A figure has appeared in the middle of a word.

9 Vegetarians has been spelt incorrectly.

10 The correct word should read mention.

11 A question mark has been used in place of an exclamation mark.

12 cc has been added but no name or extra copies have been included.

Proof Reading Practice Exercise 3

WP T

The Flora and Fauna Conservation Society

Conservation House
Henley Road
READING
RG2 6XB

Your ref ML/J6

Our ref AS/BE

(Date of typing)

Mrs Margaret Long
Thatch College
The Green
1 dorchester
Dorset
DT1 8DB

2 Dear Mrs Margaret Long

RARE PLANTS FAIR

3 Thank you for your recent letter enquiring about a Rare Plants Fayre in your area. I enclose a leaflet giving all the Fairs for this year. As you will see, the nearest ones to you will be either the one at Dyrham near Bath or the one at Ashley near Tetbury.

4 5 The Fair at Dyrham will be held on Sunday 22nd June from 10.30 am to four pm. The
6 one at Ashley Manor will be on Sat 28 June from 11 am to 5 pm.

Dyrham Park is on the A46 between Bath and the M4 Motorway. The garden has one
7 of themost elaborate water gardens in the country. A sight well worth seeing. Ashley Manor Garden is an old fashioned one nestling up to the village church. It has a
8 tradditional kitchen garden with herb terraces. You can find it on the A433 about 3 miles north east of Tetbury.

Whichever venue you decide to visit you will find many of the best specialist
9 10 nurseries inthe country. They will be selling an enourmous range of rare plants as well as some traditional varieties.

11 Whether you are a beginner or a proffesional gardener you will find something of interest to you. Expert advice will be available free of charge. Teas and refreshments will be available at both Fairs.

I hope you have an enjoyable day.

Yours faithfully

Andrew Stevens
Fair Promotions
12 —

■ Errors

1 The town should be displayed in capitals.

2 The salutation should not include the forename.

3 Inconsistent spelling of Fair.

4 Inconsistent use of punctuation for dates.

5 Inconsistent use of words and figures.

6 Failure to expand an abbreviation.

7 The space between the and most has been omitted.

8 Incorrect spelling of traditional.

9 The space between in and the has been omitted.

10 Incorrect spelling of enormous.

11 Incorrect spelling of professional.

12 Failure to indicate an enclosure.

Worked examples

Text Processing

WP T Exam Practice 1 Document 1

MODERN COMPUTING

Silicone Way
Cribbs Causeway
BRISTOL
BS8 9PU

Our ref BC/RE

Your ref GS/AC97

(Date of typing)

PERSONAL

Ms Gail Smithson
55 Potterne Road
DEVIZES
Wilts
SN10 5DQ

Dear Ms Smithson

ANNUAL CONFERENCE

Your letter addressed to Jo White has been passed to me for attention. Jo has been absent from the department for a number of days due to ill health and she is not expected back in the immediate future. I understand from your letter that you would like our company to provide a speaker for your Annual Conference to be held at the end of this year.

I am pleased to confirm that David Stone from our Personnel Office will be delighted to attend and talk on "Dealing with Stress at Work". As the conference will be spread over 2 days, David will require accommodation at the Hotel Royal in London for the Thursday night and he will travel home on Friday evening.

I will ask him to contact you direct in connection with all other details that will need to be confirmed.

Whilst looking through the outline programme for your Annual Conference I am interested to see you will have a workshop discussing the idea that "Women are Fundamental to a Successful Business". I have personally led workshops on this subject over the past few years and would be very happy to come along if you are still needing a leader. I enclose a copy of the last workshop I spoke at for your perusal.

Please contact me again if I can help in any way.

Yours sincerely

Barbara Cole
Chief Administrator

Enc

WP T Exam Practice 1 Document 2

MEMORANDUM

To David Stone

From Barbara Cole

Ref BC/RE

Date (Date of typing)

You will recall you said you would give a talk on "Dealing with Stress at Work" and I enclose herewith the correspondence I have received from Ms Gail Smithson in this connection. I have said you will contact her direct concerning all details to be confirmed and I would suggest you do this by Friday (give date for first Friday of next month) at the latest.

Ms Smithson would like a break-down of what your talk entails. Perhaps you could give her a brief outline mentioning the main areas you will cover. For example, I know you normally include such areas as identifying the causes of stress, what stress actually is and whether it can be good or bad for you.

I am sure you will include some case studies and how to adopt a personal coping strategy. From this will come an action plan including planning for your return to work if the stress factors have rendered you to have to have time off work for any period.

From the outline programme she has sent it looks to be a very interesting conference. I have said you will need accommodation on the Thursday night but you may wish to extend your stay and travel home on the Saturday. Please confirm this directly with her.

I will need to have approximate costings from you for this talk and the name of whom you would wish to deputise for you whilst you are away. Please let my secretary have this information.

Enc

WP T Exam Practice 1 Document 3

CONFERENCE VENUES

Popular venues for conferences include castles converted into hotels, country houses or even floating conference facilities on board ships. We can organise the venue to suit the conference your organisation is arranging. Below is a description of a few of our venues.

NORTH OF ENGLAND

The Castle Hotel has 20 luxuriously appointed bedrooms and is particularly suitable for high level meetings when security and privacy are important factors. Meetings can take place in the private apartments, normally the Boardroom or Library. There is also a magnificent Banqueting Hall for that all important party at the end of the conference.

In addition to a whole range of sporting activities, delegates can participate in clay pigeon shooting and archery.*

The Galaxy Centre with courtyard rooms is a specially converted conference centre comprising a mix of meeting and reception rooms. It is supported by 16 bedrooms in period cottages grouped around the Planet Courtyard. This venue is particularly suitable for training courses.

SOUTH EAST ENGLAND

Our converted 17th century tithe barn in Kent is a very versatile venue and includes:

1 all year round bookings
2 dinner dances
3 product launches
4 large or small seminars
5 exhibitions
6 day or evening bookings.

Butler's Lodge is an attractive early 18th century country house set in 50 acres of wooded parkland. It has been tastefully furnished with 28 elegant bedrooms and a delightful restaurant. The relaxed atmosphere of a large family home has been carefully maintained.

There are 3 specially equipped conference rooms for up to 60 delegates. For use in leisure time there is an open-air swimming pool within the grounds.

If London is your choice, we have the Hotel Royal as well as other hotels for you to choose from. This hotel has 300 bedrooms furnished in period style with 2 sumptuous restaurants. There are 25 conference rooms suitable for meetings of all sizes for 20 to 250 people. It has a large indoor swimming pool, sauna, solarium and a fitness centre.

* Hot-air ballooning is another option available.

2

SOUTH WEST ENGLAND

The Grand Hotel is set in tranquil gardens complete with a small lake. The hotel has 50 well-appointed bedrooms and has a French restaurant in addition to a traditional one. There are tennis courts on site and an excellent golf course in the near vicinity. Eight function rooms of varying sizes are available.

The Royal Oak, set in the centre of a 100-acre park, has 170 bedrooms and 9 meeting rooms for between 10 and 250 people. On site leisure facilities include tennis courts, bowls, croquet and a 27-hole golf course.

Water Castle is a splendid stone castle situated close to Dartmoor. It has 45 finely furnished bedrooms and there are conference facilities for up to 60 delegates. <u>Among the leisure pursuits is pony trekking.</u>

SAILING CONFERENCES

We have 3 ships for you to bear in mind if you want to organise an event with a difference.

> You can sail to Holland, Calais, Dieppe or cruise the Irish Sea routes. Our largest ship has a 250 seat auditorium and our smallest has space for up to 50 people. You can combine lunch in Calais with a half-day programme meeting. The possibilities are endless.**

All our venues are complete with the necessary business aids you will need. Fax machines and photocopiers are available throughout the duration of your booking.

Business and pleasure do go together. Leisure time is very important, that is why it is high on our list of priorities.

March 1997

** Contact our sailing conference department for details.

WP T Exam Practice 2 Document 1

THE TOY
CHEST

Head Office
63 Newall Road
HARROGATE
York
YO1 2NE

Our ref MICKT/P/KP/GC

Your ref KP/SM

(Date of typing)

FOR THE ATTENTION OF MRS K PETERSON

50 Combe Park
ST IVES
Cornwall
TR42 1BY

Dear Mrs Peterson

MICROSCOPE KIT

Thank you for your recent letter. We are sorry to learn of your disappointment in our microscope kit you purchased for your son's birthday.

The kit is one of our most popular products and we have sold over 5,000 sets this year. As this is a high quality product we rarely receive any complaints regarding this kit and were therefore surprised to receive your comments. The kit was examined by a member of our staff and we agree that this particular item is faulty. The kit has now been returned to the manufacturers for their comments.

As stated in our catalogue, we guarantee all our merchandise will reach you in perfect condition. Clearly we did not fulfil our guarantee on this occasion. We are therefore enclosing with this letter a cheque for £80 made up as follows. The full price of the microscope kit of £65, together with a refund of £5 for postage costs incurred in returning this product. A further £10 has been added to compensate you for the disappointment and inconvenience you have suffered.

We hope that this incident will not prevent you from ordering from us in the future. We are enclosing a copy of our latest catalogue for your perusal.

We look forward to hearing from you.

Yours sincerely

Gary Carter
Manager

Enc

WP T Exam Practice 2 Document 2

MEMORANDUM

To Laura Paige

From Gary Carter

Ref MICKT/P/KP/GC

Date (Date of typing)

Faulty Microscope Kit

I attach a copy of a letter received from Mrs Peterson from which you will see the microscope kit was in fact faulty. I have returned the kit to the manufacturers and am waiting for an explanation as to how this kit passed through their checking procedures.

Obviously, all the toys we sell must conform to toy safety regulations. The local Trading Standards Officer visits head office regularly. Any items that do not meet the rigorous safety standards are immediately withdrawn from sale.

To avoid this potentially embarrassing situation, please instigate a check on the stockroom for these kits, and remove any that have the same batch number. Please issue a memo to all branch managers requesting they check their stock. Give a deadline of Monday of next week, (insert date).

Depending on the explanation received from the manufacturers we may have to source another supplier of these items. I cannot remember seeing any microscopes at the recent trade exhibitions. Please check the latest editions of the scientific equipment catalogues. As this is one of our best-selling items, we must be sure of maintaining our stock levels.

The current trade price of the microscope kit is £35 plus VAT. Unfortunately, this is a low margin item. We cannot afford to pay more than £38 plus VAT per unit without affecting the retail price.

Enc

Exam Practice 2 Document 3

European Communities Commission - Directive on Toy Safety

On 1 January 1990, a Directive was issued to ensure the same level of toy safety throughout the European Community.

Dangerous toys can be due to mechanical failure, manufacturing errors or unsuitable materials. However slight the hazard, it can cause serious injury to a small child. The safety of any toy not only depends on its manufacture, but also on its design.

Adults also have a responsibility to ensure children use the toys for their specific purpose. Allowing children to mishandle toys can turn a safe toy into a potentially hazardous item.

In order to prevent and reduce the number of accidents, each of the following groups has a part to play.

1 The manufacturers
2 The importers
3 The retailers
4 The users and their carers

Young children and babies love to touch, smell or taste different objects. This means that the material and substances used in the manufacture of play items must be completely harmless.

2

The "CE" Mark

The "CE" mark or label attached to toys means that the item meets the requirements laid down in the Directive.

This mark must be affixed to the toy or its packaging. It must be visible, indelible and easily legible. If an item is too small for the mark to be affixed, it may be displayed on the packaging or on a separate leaflet.

Manufacturers must ensure that their products are designed and manufactured in line with the requirements set out in the Directive. Items must conform with the standards set by the European Committee for Standardisation (CEN) and the European Committee for Electrotechnical Standardisation (CENELEC).* Conformity will provide sufficient evidence to presume that the toy has complied with the regulations of the Directive.

Importers, distributors and wholesalers must not sell toys unless they carry the CE mark. The purchaser should check the toys bear the CE mark. The manufacturers' name and address or that of their authorised representative should also be stated on the toy or packaging.

* These bodies set detailed technical specifications and decide test methods.

WP T

Exam Practice 2 Document 3 (continued)

3

The user also has a responsibility to ensure the toy is used as intended in accordance with the manufacturer's instructions.** They must ensure that the recommended minimum age is respected and use the item in accordance with instructions.

The Member States must carry out checks on toys offered for sale and prohibit or restrict any that falsely carry the CE mark. They may also prohibit the sale of toys that are <u>likely</u> to endanger the health and safety of the user.

In the UK, the Government office responsible for these checks is the Trading Standards Office.

Physical and Mechanical Requirements

The Directive outlines the physical and mechanical properties which toys must display if they are to qualify for the CE mark. There are a number of rules which must be adhered to.

Generally toys must be suitable for the purpose for which they were intended. They must be strong and stable enough to withstand stresses. Toys and their packaging must not present a risk of strangulation or suffocation.

** As the user is probably a minor, then the adult responsible for supervision must take this responsibility.

4

Chemical Requirements

As well as the physical and mechanical requirements, there are also rules on the chemical requirements of toys.

Generally they must not present any risks of poisoning or physical injury by coming into contact with the child's skin, mucous membranes or eyes.

Flammability

All toys must be manufactured from materials that are not readily flammable.

Further information can be obtained from the Official Journal of the European Communities No L 187.

WP T Exam Practice 3 Document 1

Homecare Supplies

Homecare House
Wells Road
READING
RG1 3XW

Our ref PE/SV

Your ref PM/546

(Date of Typing)

Mrs P Miller
49 Marsh Street
READING
RG2 8WL

Dear Mrs Miller

CARING FOR THE ELDERLY

Thank you for your letter received today for information on our new caring aids for the elderly. We have been working closely with various other manufacturers who specialise in these aids and our work together has been very worthwhile.

You will see from the enclosed catalogue, simple adaptations in the home can ease pain and make life generally easier all round. Some of these simple modifications will mean life will be made easier for you too.

The following points will be useful to put to your next committee meeting. The complex you are responsible for includes rooms upstairs as well as on the level. A handrail on both sides of the stairs is a must. To avoid falling over unexpected objects, we recommend a well lit hall, landing and stairway with a two-way switch upstairs as well as downstairs.

As you still have baths and not showers in your rooms, ensure you have all the necessary handrails fitted. These should be fixed to either the walls or the floor to ensure they give good support when getting in or out of the bath. If your committee is planning new bathrooms, it might be better for them to consider fitting a shower unit. This should be one that can be walked into or even allow access for a wheelchair. Special seats can also be fitted in showers.

We look forward to hearing from you again.

Yours sincerely

Paul Edwards
Care Consultant

Enc

WP T Exam Practice 3 Document 2

MEMORANDUM

To Timothy North

From Paul Edwards

Ref PE/SV

Date (Date of typing)

URGENT

I have received the enclosed letter from Mrs Miller in which she asks for information on our caring aids. You will note that she states that the complex she is warden for has no shower facilities. The complex is a large one on two floors with accommodation for 50 people in single rooms. At the present time there is a bathroom shared between every 4 rooms. Each single room has a wash basin only.

She is putting forward at her next committee meeting the possibility of having en suite facilities to include shower cubicles for all rooms. There is space for this work to be done without making the living area of each room too small. They will keep the remaining bathrooms but the facilities will need upgrading.

Perhaps you could look at this as a matter of urgency and go to see Mrs Miller as soon as possible. You can then discuss with her exactly what her requirements will be. It will also be a good opportunity for you to advise her on the approximate cost of all the work.

The existing bathrooms may only need minor adjustments made or they may require to be completely refurbished. Look at what handrails and shelves are there. All taps will need to have lever type handles.

Try to make an appointment to see her on (give date for first Monday of next month).

Enc

WP T

Exam Practice 3 Document 3

PRESERVING WINTER WARMTH

As a company working towards the well-being of the elderly we have the following hints for preserving winter warmth. These should be issued to all people living in warden controlled care, as well as those living in their own properties.

To some extent everyone is at risk from illness in very cold weather. Avoid taking unnecessary risks and ensure you keep warm. Food and drink are essential fuel for the body. During very cold weather, eat at least one hot meal per day and have as many hot drinks as you can. They will help to make you feel warmer inside.

A hot drink before going to bed will help you to keep warm. Keep a vacuum flask filled with a hot drink at your bedside as this will help if you wake up in the night feeling cold.

Eat plenty of fresh fruit and vegetables when you are able to. Remember that bread, milk, potatoes, meat and fish* are all excellent sources of protein, vitamins and energy.

Other key points for keeping well and warm are:

1 keep a constant temperature in all rooms
2 make sure your home is well insulated
3 use draught excluders and keep curtains closed
4 have a little exercise each day if possible
5 wrap up well before going out, wear a hat, gloves and scarf
6 keep warm in bed at night.

A WARM HOME

A comfortably warm home should be your aim at all times. At night the temperature can fall particularly low and so it is best to sleep with windows closed in cold weather. A wall thermometer is a useful way to check on how warm your rooms are.

A hot water bottle is a simple and cheap way of adding extra warmth both in the day and at night. Never use a hot water bottle in bed if you have an electric blanket. Wear warm night wear and bed socks whilst in bed.

HOME INSULATION

All the heat in your home will eventually flow out through windows, ceilings, floors and doors. Keep your home well insulated and draught proof where you can especially around windows. Hang a heavy curtain over the front door and get a letter box cover. Curtains with thermal linings all help to keep draughts out.

* Poultry, eggs, cheese and nuts are other good sources of protein.

2

KEEPING ACTIVE

To avoid circulation problems, move about indoors if you are not able to get outside for some exercise. In very cold and icy weather it is better to stay indoors. Walk up and down stairs if you have them. This helps to exercise your whole body.

When you do go outside wear warm underwear and several light layers of clothing under your coat. Wear a scarf, gloves and a hat at all times outside.

It is also important to wear strong, warm shoes or boots. An extra pair of socks** will help if your shoes or boots are roomy enough.

GENERAL CARE

When having a bath or shower, do not take too long and avoid letting the water get cold. If taking a bath ensure it has the necessary handrails fitted for your safety.

> Depending on your financial circumstances you may be able to get a grant to help with loft insulation and draught proofing for doors and windows.

There are also some budget schemes available for you to pay for your fuel more easily. Contact our energy department for further details.

March 1997

** A warm insole can be added to insulate your feet against the cold.

WP T Exam Practice 4 Document 1

Somerset Local Authority
Town Hall
SHEPTON MALLET
Somerset
SH8 0NE

Our Ref PC/DM/63985.1

Your Ref PC/LK/DO2.1

(Date of typing)

Mrs Paula Carter
Rose Cottage
Watery Lane
SHEPTON MALLET
Somerset
SM4 6QZ

Dear Mrs Carter

COUNCIL RECYCLING INITIATIVE

Thank you for your recent letter expressing concern at the lack of recycling facilities in this area. I am pleased to inform you that the local authority is just about to launch a recycling initiative in this area. Full details of this initiative will be published shortly.

Basically, the scheme will provide for many recyclable materials to be collected from residents' homes. Special plastic boxes will be issued to each household so that the materials can be stored separately. It is hoped that the scheme, which will be on a trial basis, will prove to be very successful. It could save the council over £250,000 each year. This does not take into account other benefits such as saving the energy used in the production of these materials and the conservation of natural resources.

Other measures the Environmental Committee are considering include reducing pollution in town centres and offering a free collection service for discarded refrigerators.

Out of town park and ride schemes are being built on the outskirts of the busiest town centres in the area. Public transport will ferry commuters to the centre. This service will be provided at a very small charge. It is hoped that this service will prevent commuters from bringing their vehicles into the town centre. This would reduce congestion and pollution.

I am enclosing a copy of our Environmental Policy booklet. If you would like any further information, please let me know.

Yours sincerely

Joseph Daniels
Environmental Officer

Enc

WP T Exam Practice 4 Document 2

MEMORANDUM

To Lucy Patterson

From Joseph Daniels

Ref JD/LP/629

Date (Date of typing)

URGENT

Recycling Initiative

I am attaching a copy of a letter I have sent to a Mrs Carter. She has expressed concern at the lack of recycling facilities in the area. I hope that the scheme will be extremely successful. Mrs Carter's letter is typical of many I have received in recent months.

We must get the publicity and promotional materials ready for the launch next month. I am attaching some notes for the leaflet that will be delivered to each household. It clearly sets out how to use the collection boxes.

In order to raise awareness of this initiative, I would like you to start planning the launch. My ideas include holding a recycling exhibition at the town hall or having a party in the park. We could also involve local school children in some way. This could be a colouring competition with the winning entry being used as a poster or leaflet design. It could form the cover of the recycling leaflet. Local traders could be approached to donate prizes for this event.

Perhaps you could consider some of these ideas and devise some of your own. Please remember that we have a very small budget so any events must be inexpensive to run. Let me have your thoughts by Tuesday (insert date) of next week.

Encs

WP T Exam Practice 4 Document 3

Council Recycling Initiative

As part of the Council's firm commitment to recycling, a collection service for reusable materials will be set up. This new service will be on a trial basis for six months.

It is very much hoped that the public will respond to this important initiative. The success of our scheme relies on your co-operation.

In order to help you collect your materials, the Council will provide you with a collection box. This will be delivered to each household within the next few weeks. These boxes are designed for use by an average sized household, however smaller boxes can be provided upon request.

If you do not want to participate in this scheme, please contact the Council. Arrangements will be made for your box to be collected from your home.

All waste materials that are collected will be used for recycling. This will help conserve natural resources and reduce the energy used in manufacturing these materials. The Council estimates that over £250,000 can be saved each year by the sale of these materials. This will benefit the whole community.

The items that can be accepted for recycling are:

1 Newspapers and magazines
2 Glass jars and bottles
3 Food and drink cans
4 Aluminium foil
5 Car batteries
6 Oil filters and sump oil
7 Clothes, shoes and rags

It would assist our staff if you could follow these simple guidelines when leaving your waste materials for collection.

<u>Newspapers and Magazines</u>

These should be kept in a separate bundle and placed on top of your box. The bundle should be securely tied to prevent the papers blowing away.

Please do not include telephone directories or cardboard[1]. These are not suitable for recycling.

[1] A separate bank for cardboard is situated at the Avon Road refuse tip.

WP T Exam Practice 4 Document 3 (continued)

3

Glass Jars and Bottles

These should be placed directly in the box. Please ensure they have been rinsed before discarding. Remove lids and corks as these cannot be used.

Unfortunately, we cannot accept window glass or toughened glass used to make tableware or cookware. **Obviously, we cannot handle broken glass.** There is no need to separate bottles and jars into different colours.

Drink and Food Cans

We can collect steel and aluminium cans. These include food, drinks and pet food cans. Lids should be removed completely and placed inside the tin. Those with jagged edges should not be put out for collection. Please ensure that cans have been rinsed thoroughly. Dirty cans are unhygenic and may cause a health hazard.

Aluminium Foil

This must be placed in a separate bag.[2] We can only accept clean foil. Plastic or paper backed foil, ie chocolate wrappers, is not acceptable.

Car Batteries

These should be placed alongside your collection box. They should not be left outside your property until collection day. When handling car batteries, please be careful. Remember, the battery contains acid which could be harmful if spilt.

[2] It is helpful if you collect a full bag of foil before leaving for collection.

4

Oil Filters and Sump Oil

Oil filters should be drained. Ensure the filter is covered in a plastic bag. This will help prevent oil leaking.

Sump oil should be placed in a clean, sealed container. Sump oil and filters should not be left on the kerbside until collection day.

Clothes, Shoes and Rags

Shoes should be tied together in pairs. Clothes and rags should be clean. These items must be placed in a separate bag and kept dry.

The collections will take place each week. However, they will be on a different day to your normal refuse collection. Bank holiday arrangements will be published in the local newspaper.

If you encounter any problems with the collections, please call our Recycling Helpline on 01632 696969.

WP T Exam Practice 5 Document 1

Home Design 2000

Unit 4
Park Nurseries Estate
BATH
BA2 4JH

Our ref JM/BE

Your ref SW/Home

(Date of typing)

Mr Stewart Wright
41 Empire Crescent
LEAMINGTON SPA
Warwickshire
CV31 2XP

Dear Mr Wright

HEARTS AND FLOWERS THEME

Thank you for your recent letter enquiring about our latest promotion. For the month of February our company will create an easy and lively look for one of your rooms using our hearts and flowers theme. The cost will depend on the size of your room and the accessories you decide to use.

It can be very difficult to know where to begin when you are decorating a room from scratch. Our experts will advise you on which element to make your starting point. You may decide to use a colour from our range of curtain fabric as your basis to work from. This year the colours are strong. Yellow, green and blue together with terracotta are the main ones. Many of the fabrics include the current hearts and flowers motif, which is the theme for this year.

In connection with your request for information on our designs for adapting a room suitable for use as an office at home, we enclose our current catalogue. You will see that the essential elements are a desk, chair and storage items. Again our experts will be able to give you ideas on the best layout for your room when they visit your home.

You can continue the hearts and flowers theme in your office by adding heart-shaped silk or velvet cushions to your small sofa. The size of your room will dictate what furniture you will have space for.

A representative from our Design Department will be in touch with you within the next few days.

Yours sincerely

Jeremy Matthews
Sales Manager

Enc

WP T Exam Practice 5 Document 2

MEMORANDUM

To	Andrew Milsome
From	Jeremy Matthews
Ref	JM/BE
Date	(Date of typing)

URGENT

We have received a good response to our February promotion and I enclose a letter from Mr Wright for you to respond to. Mr Wright would like his teenage daughter's bedroom created in the hearts and flowers theme. You will need to make an appointment with him to see the room and I would suggest you do this as soon as possible. The (give date for first Monday of next month) would be best as I would be free to go with you.

We will need to check the size of the room, placement of windows and door etc. I understand Mr Wright does not wish to purchase new furniture. He only requires re-decoration, new curtains and bed linen. He is willing to buy a few small accessories for the room. The carpet is pale pink and as it is quite new, we will need to co-ordinate our colours around it. I foresee no problems with this job.

Whilst at the house Mr Wright would like us to look at the possibility of fitting a work station in the recess under the stairs. He would like one that can be disguised as a cupboard when not in use.

We will need to have an idea of the approximate cost of this before we go.

Enc

WP T Exam Practice 5 Document 3

HOME IMPROVEMENT AND DECORATION

More and more people are going to work without actually stepping outside the door. By the beginning of the next century it is estimated that over five million people will be working from home. The three essential elements needed are a desk, chair and storage equipment.

FURNITURE

Your desk should suit the equipment you will be using. A desk space arranged in an L-shape would be best if you have a computer, a fax, telephone and other miscellaneous items. It is necessary to have your desk near a natural source of light and your computer at an angle to the window to reduce the glare.

You should be able to sit comfortably at your desk with your knees under it. Some have drawers to one side which are useful for storage space.*

Never compromise by making do with a chair from the dining room. Your ideal chair should include the following:

1 lumber support to avoid back pains
2 swivel action for easy movement
3 adjustable seat

* Trestle tables are a cheaper alternative to desks.

2

4 arm supports
5 castors to avoid over stretching
6 height adjustment.

Organise an efficient filing system before you have papers piling up. Have the things you use most frequently close at hand. Consider what you have to store and put papers in filing boxes or a filing cabinet. Shelves or drawers are useful storage for other things.

ROOM BLENDING

Many furniture designers are realising that space is at a premium in most homes. Office furniture may end up in a room that is regularly used by the family. For this reason it is very important that it should blend in with the existing surroundings.

The dining room and the guest room are the most popular places to set up a home office as these rooms are not usually in constant use. Choose a desk and chair that blend or co-ordinate with your existing decoration.

Cover any files or binders with a fabric to match your curtains. Use a screen to hide your office furniture. You could cover the screen in a fabric to match your room and this would be an ideal way of screening off your work area.

MAKING SPACE

You can create your own office in an alcove or even a recess under the stairs. Divide your largest room into two sections using versatile backless book shelves.** Use roller blinds or sliding doors to close off office space in alcoves and recesses when not in use.

** These can be combined to create numerous shapes.

WP T Exam Practice 5 Document 3 (continued)

3

DECORATION

All the very strong colours are very popular this year. As well as yellow, green and blue you can choose the colour terracotta to have as a textured cover for your soft furnishings. The overall effect of bold colours makes a strong statement to your room. Use lighter shades for cushions, vases and other accessories. Choose pastel shades for walls and ceiling if using bold colours for furniture.

> February, being traditionally known as the romantic month of the year, is the time to decorate using pastel shades. A combination of pale blue and white can bring a touch of romance to a room. White voile cross-over curtains filter the light at a window. Scattered rose design bed linen and rose gingham drapes all add to the effect. Heart-shaped picture frames and mirrors or clocks are the ideal accessories.

Flowers add the final touch to any room. During spring, tulips are the most colourful and varied seasonal flower around. They are easy to work with and make wonderful arrangements.

March 1997

WP T Exam Practice 6 Document 1

GRANGE BANK PLC
1 High Street
HASTINGS
E Sussex
HT1 6YV

Our ref CN/AD/139.6.2

Your ref BM/CR

(Date of typing)

Mr C Norris
51 Battlefield Hill Road
HASTINGS
E Sussex
HT1 3QD

Dear Mr Norris

BANKING SERVICES

Thank you for your recent letter enquiring about our banking services. I am pleased to enclose a copy of our brochure entitled 'Banking in the 90s'. This brochure contains detailed explanations of all our banking services.

I gather from your letter that you are dissatisfied with the level of customer service provided by your current bankers. We pride ourselves on our excellent customer service at Grange Bank plc. All our staff are fully trained in all aspects of our range of products and services. When you join our bank you will be assigned to a personal banker. You can call them direct with any problems or query you may have.

The law dictates that any financial advice we give must remain impartial. We feel we offer the best independent financial advice around. We have our own mortgage consultants, stockbrokers and insurance brokers who will be pleased to discuss any aspect of their specialist areas with you. Should you decide to place your business with us after talking to our specialists, you can be assured of a fast, professional service.

Please take the time to read our brochure. We are sure you will be impressed with the range of products and services we offer. If, after reading our literature, you require any further information, please do not hesitate to contact me.

Yours sincerely

Andrew Dalton
Branch Manager

Enc

WP T Exam Practice 6 Document 2

MEMORANDUM

To Martin Winters

From Andrew Dalton

Ref CP/AD/1396.1

Date (Date of typing)

CONFIDENTIAL

I attach a copy of a letter received from a Mr C Norris. As you can see, he is not satisfied with the level of service he is receiving from his current bankers. I am delighted that he chose to write to us requesting details of our services. A copy of my reply is also attached.

This is not the first customer who has decided to transfer their business to us. It appears that some of our competitors in the district are losing custom because of poor customer service. Where possible, we should take these opportunities to increase business.

A new advertising campaign should be launched. The emphasis should be on our caring attitude towards our customers. Perhaps we could combine this with the wide range of financial services we offer. The campaign could be on the lines of "Everyone is happy at Grange Bank plc". We could show different customers each with a different financial problem.

Obviously the large-scale advertising campaigns are produced and devised by advertising agents employed by head office. However, local branches are able to put together small-scale relevant advertising that meets local needs. The proposal for such an advertising campaign must be submitted to head office before any advertising can be booked.

Please put together some ideas for a local campaign. A written proposal must accompany any draft advertisements. You will also need to find out the costs for advertising in the local newspaper.

I would like to have your proposal by next Wednesday (insert date) at the latest.

Encs

WP T Exam Practice 6 Document 3

Banking in the 90s

Banking has come a long way from the days when only the rich had bank accounts. In the past, banking halls were quiet, formal places. People spoke in hushed voices and speed of service was unheard of.

Customers were treated with the utmost respect. However, it was felt that the manager and staff were unapproachable. Women rarely had their own bank accounts. Generally, a single working woman had to ask a male relative to guarantee her financial affairs before she was allowed to open an account.

Grange Bank plc still treats its customers with respect. Each customer is seen as an individual. Whatever your needs, whatever your problem, come and talk to us. We are confident we will be able to provide a solution.

The services offered by Grange Bank plc have also moved with the times. You can bring all your financial needs to us. Book an appointment with our specialists. The consultation is free of charge.

We can provide a wide range of services including:

1 Current accounts
2 Savings plans
3 Pension plans
4 Travel services
5 Deposit accounts
6 Student accounts
7 Mortgages
8 Share dealing

WP T

Exam Practice 6 Document 3 (continued)

2

Current Account

Customers who keep their accounts in credit do not pay any charges. If you are transferring your account from another bank we ask for a reference. Provided this is satisfactory, we will issue you with a cheque guarantee card and cashpoint card straightaway.* If you have not held an account before then we will issue a cheque guarantee card and cashpoint card after three months' satisfactory banking.

Once your account has been established we will agree an overdraft facility with you. This will give you peace of mind should you have an unexpected expense.

Travel Services

If you are travelling abroad, whether on business or taking the holiday of a lifetime, Grange Bank plc offers many services.

We can help with traveller's cheques, insurance, Eurocard and foreign currency. The commission rates for foreign currency are very competitive. We can supply most currencies without prior notice. Our traveller's insurance policies will ensure peace of mind whilst travelling aboard, however long your stay.

* For customers who have their salary paid into their current account, a cheque guarantee card of up to £100 can be issued.

3

Deposit Accounts

For those who require instant access to their money, our deposit accounts attract an excellent rate of interest. These are suitable for clubs and societies to use.**

Pension Plans

It is never too early to start planning for your retirement. On average you will need a pension of at least half your final annual salary. Our pensions adviser will be able to give you the best independent advice available. Should you decide to take out a personal pension plan, we are confident you will find ours are among the best performers on the market.

Mortgages

Endowment, pension, repayment or PEP, the choice is wide and can be confusing. Our mortgage experts will help you unravel this complicated area. Whether you would like a capped, fixed or variable rate, you will find our mortgages are flexible.

Grange Bank plc does not believe in gimmicks and you won't find us offering large discounts or cashback. However, unlike most other lenders we do not tie you down by making you stay with us for a long period. **Large penalties for early redemption are not imposed on our borrowers.**

** We also have a special account for clubs and societies. Please ask for further details.

WP T Exam Practice 6 Document 3 (continued)

4

Share Dealing

Grange Bank plc provides a comprehensive share dealing and portfolio administration service. Our specialists in this area can advise you on the performance of your shares.

We can give you 24 hours a day access to your portfolio so that you can make an informed investment decision.   Each quarter we will send you a full portfolio valuation so that you can see exactly how your investments are performing.

These are just a few of the services we offer, call in at your local branch to find out more about us. Our staff will be delighted to help you.

WP Exam Practice 1 Document 1

BUYING AND SELLING A PROPERTY

MOVING HOUSE

Moving house is one of life's most stressful events. Experts rate it as the third most stressful happening. It is just below the death of a spouse or divorce.

Whilst it is recognised that moving house is difficult, you can take steps to ensure your move goes as smoothly as possible.

Choosing an Estate Agency

What to look for

Once you have decided to move, your first step is to register your property with an estate agent. Look in your local newspaper or property paper to find some companies. Ask family and friends if they can recommend a reputable agency.

By following these guidelines you should be able to choose a reputable agent.

Before you decide check the following:

1 Does the agency advertise in the local paper regularly?
2 Are the property details they prepare accurate and interesting?
3 Do they take colour photographs of your house?
4 Will your property details be held at each of their branches?
5 Are the staff enthusiastic and motivated?

Art.SL5.931.2

2

BUYING AND SELLING A PROPERTY

The Valuation

It is a good idea to ask at least three local companies to value your property. Make sure that they will provide this service free of charge. This should give you a realistic idea of how much your house may fetch. It may not be the best idea to register with the agency that quotes a very high figure. This may mean your property will take a long time to sell.

Try to find out what other properties the agency has sold in your area in recent months. Beware of agents who tell you they can sell your property in a very short period of time.

Commission

Ask each agency how much commission it charges. The difference in fees between agencies can mean large savings for you. It is usual for the commission charge to be approximately 2% - 3% of the puchase price. If you register with just one agent, and agree to keep your property with them for a specified period, they may offer a discount. Registering with 2 or more agencies will add another ½% - 1% to their commission charges.

Art.SL5.931.2

WP Exam Practice 1 Document 1 (continued)

3

BUYING AND SELLING A PROPERTY

<u>Viewings</u>

A good agency will be keen to arrange as many viewings as possible. Check that an agent will accompany prospective purchasers, particularly if you are in your house alone. Make it clear that you will not receive viewers unless they have previously arranged an appointment.

Generally, estate agencies will not allow you to arrange viewings privately. If you sell your property through a friend or relative, you will still be liable to pay your agent their commission.

Art.SL5.931.2

4

BUYING AND SELLING A PROPERTY

<u>Property Details</u>

When the agent arrives to measure your property, spend some time with them discussing the best features of your house. Point out any work you have undertaken, particularly central heating, a new roof, re-wiring etc. If your house has any interesting features these should be stated on the property details.

Ensure that you check the details before they are sent out to prospective purchasers. Ask for details to be changed if you feel they are inaccurate or do not make the best of your house.

By following these guidelines you should be able to choose a reputable agent.

Aty.SI.5.931.2

WP Exam Practice 1 Document 2

Current Potential Purchasers - August

Name	Telephone Number	Requirements	Price £ Thousands
Mr and Mrs Phipps	01289 378292	3 bed period property, garage and garden	80 - 90
Miss Northedge	01289 379265	1 - 2 bed flat, central location	40 - 50
Mr Carter	01684 844126	4 bed semi-detached house, large garden, must have double garage	150 - 200
Mr Janson	01354 213196	3 bed semi, post 1920, garden	70 - 80
Mr and Mrs Bally	01694 886621	2 bed bungalow, must be on bus route	65 - 80
Ms Kennett	01354 298776	2 bed house, must be in good order	55 - 80
Mr and Mrs Singh	01289 367543	4 bed terrace, must be near Jordan School	90 - 100
Mr and Mrs Murphy	01354 542193	4 bed house, prepared to renovate	70 - 85
Mr Peters	01289 354432	1 bed flat, in good order	45 - 48

Properties Registered in August

Property Address	Outline Descrition	Price £ Thousands
45 Queen Road, Bath	2 bedroom house, small garden	50
32 Edward Avenue, Bath	3 bedroom semi-detached house, garden, double garage	78
91 Waltham Place, Chippenham	4 bedroom, modern detached house, garden, double garage	85
7 Golden Street, Bath	2 bedroom terrace, needs improvement	42
25 Chaucer Lane, Bath	1 bedroom flat in excellent decorative order	45

WP Exam Practice 1 Document 3

ADVERTISEMENT FEATURE

PHOENIX PROPERTY AGENCY

Phoenix Property Agency has been trading successfully in this area for 21 years. Its distinctive blue and yellow signs are a familiar sight throughout the region. Phoenix signs can be seen selling flats, houses, bungalows and even manor houses.

The Branch Manager, William Fitzgerald, stated: "Phoenix Property Agency has survived the housing recession because of its caring and professional approach to selling property. Clients know they will receive a first-class service from staff who are motivated to sell their property. We pride ourselves on our high standards of customer care."

Phoenix Property Agency has 17 branches throughout the region and can be found in local community areas as well as high streets. For increased customer convenience, many of our branches are attached to a Phoenix Building Society.

Buying and selling property can often be fraught with difficulties. The financial help offered by Phoenix Building Society can go a long way to making this difficult time much easier. Financial services include mortgages, pensions, PEPS, property and home contents insurance.

Once a property has been registered, a member of staff will visit your property to take measurements. Attractive full-colour property details are prepared and sent to all branches in the region. The details are also added to our extensive database where they will be matched with prospective buyers' requirements. Regular, full-colour advertisements are taken in local newspapers each week.

To celebrate 21 years in business, Phoenix Property Agency is offering clients the chance to sell their property for only 1% commission. Of course, the usual 'no sale, no fee' guarantee applies.

To take advantage of this marvellous deal, all you need to do is register your property for sale with Phoenix Property Agency during the month of September.

WP Exam Practice 1 Document 4

MEMORANDUM

To Matthew Soames

From Carole Hill

Ref MS/CA/MD

Date (Date of typing)

29 LYME AVENUE

This property has been placed with us by Mr and Mrs Dinning. It is a semi-detached house with garage and is in excellent decorative order. The property comprises 3 large bedrooms, family bathroom, lounge, dining room, study and luxury kitchen/breakfast room. The master bedroom has an en-suite shower. The garden is large and contains:

Greenhouse
Lawns
Patio
Rockery
Vegetable plot

The purchase price is to be in the region of £97,000.

The current owners need to sell the property quickly as they have found a house they wish to buy. Please ensure the details are prepared immediately and distributed to all branches in the region.

The details must be typed as soon as possible and certainly no later than 3 days. The client should receive a copy to check before any are sent out.

Property details must also be sent to suitable prospective buyers who are on our mailing database. Please ensure that the buying requirements are carefully matched and checked. This will ensure we do not annoy clients by sending them information on properties that are not suitable for them.

I am pleased we have been asked to deal with the sale of this property as it is outside of our usual area. If we can find a buyer within a couple of weeks, we may be able to secure more business from this part of the city.

Copies Paul Williams
File

Copies Paul Williams ✓
File

Copies Paul Williams
File ✓

WP Exam Practice 2 Document 1

WORLD HOLIDAYS

Holidays are something that everyone looks forward to. This last year has shown an increase in more breaks being taken in this country than for many years.

We need to advertise and attract more people to our holidays both at home and abroad if we are to maintain our profit levels.

> Our brochures for this season are now available for distribution. The opening page states how our holidays all include full board, free wine with meals, activities, entertainment and excursions. Tourists will require money to cover their own personal expenses and any optional excursions.

We have a wide choice of destinations in Great Britain, Europe and the Mediterranean. The hotels we use range from large ones with plenty of accommodation and organised entertainment to small family-run ones with a somewhat quieter atmosphere. At most resorts we offer a varied programme of activities. Car hire is available. We need to stress the importance of these points when talking to prospective holiday-makers.

1997 SEASON

WP Exam Practice 2 Document 1 (continued)

WORLD HOLIDAYS

Self-catering is an alternative.

Self-catering holidays are for those who wish to have a carefree break, where their time will be their own.

We have many apartments in a variety of resorts. Whether one or two bedroom apartments, each will have a separate lounge, kitchen area and bathroom. The facilities in each include the following:

Cooking utensils

Crockery

Cutlery

Fridge

Hairdryer

Iron and ironing board

Linen and towels

Maid service

Oven and cooking rings

Telephone

1997 SEASON 2

WORLD HOLIDAYS

Self-catering holidays are for those who wish to have a carefree break, where their time will be their own.

Explain when booking these that linen and towels will be changed each week and that all apartments have heating, gas and electricity. These are included in the price.

Coach tours at home and abroad are still very popular. All tours are accompanied by a courier. Our coaches are well upholstered for a comfortable ride. For the additional comfort of passengers, there is no smoking and no loud intrusive music on all coaches. We need to advertise for more couriers for our French tours.

> New to our itinerary this year is a tour which includes a leisurely cruise for holiday-makers to enjoy. They can discover the classical sites of Greece on a tour combined with a cruise around the Greek Islands. This is sure to be a very attractive addition to our brochure.

1997 SEASON 3

WP Exam Practice 2 Document 2

RESORT HOLIDAYS 1997

Resort	Amenities	Departure Date	Duration (nights)	Price Per Person £
Corfu Crete Rhodes Tenerife Isle of Lewis Harrogate	Outdoor swimming pool with sun terrace and sunbeds Games room with snooker tables and table tennis Poolside bar, gift shop and air-conditioning throughout TV room, mini golf Vegetarian diets provided Excursions to York Minster, Ripon Cathedral and Fountains Abbey	1 September 29 April 7 May 27 May 7 June 23 December	7 7 14 21 7 4	475 395 599 695 315 295

VERONA OPERA FESTIVAL

Title	Brief Details of Opera	Tour Details
Carmen Madam Butterfly Macbeth	Bizet's tragic tale set in Seville Puccini's tragic story of a young Japanese girl A popular Verdi opera	Choose from a 5, 6 or 7-night tour staying in hotels on the shores of Lake Garda. An excursion to Venice can be included.

WP Exam Practice 2 Document 1 (continued)

WORLD HOLIDAYS

Special interest breaks are always well booked. This year we have added a visit to a banana plantation and botanical garden whilst on our "Gardens in Tenerife" break.

A hiking holiday in the Derbyshire Dales with an experienced guide will allow walkers to experience the peace and tranquillity of the Dales.

If any member of your staff can achieve a 10% increase in holidays to resorts on the Western Isles, they will receive a free 2-day break there for two.

1997 SEASON 4

WP Exam Practice 2 Document 3

BOATING HOLIDAYS FOR ALL AGES

Boating holidays will appeal to all age groups. It is a relaxing and different holiday away from all the everyday cares of life.

Discover Britain along the winding rivers and canals. Cruise along these picturesque waterways at a gentle pace. Go ashore at your leisure whenever you wish and explore countryside villages and historic towns.

You will have opportunities to fish, cycle or just walk through beautiful countryside. You can moor alongside waterside inns and restaurants.

SELECT A HOLIDAY FROM THE FOLLOWING PARTS OF THE COUNTRY.

The Norfolk Broads

Miles and miles of idyllic boating through this conservation area. This area of water is lock-free and so you can meander along at a leisurely pace, admiring the wildlife and listening to the birdsong around you.

Visit the beautiful city of Norwich with its two cathedrals and a castle.

Kennet and Avon Canal

From Bristol to London this canal will take you through rural England and give you an opportunity to experience the industrial heritage of the waterway for yourself.

Stratford-upon-Avon

On the River Avon you can moor opposite the Royal Shakespeare Theatre.

Spend time looking around Stratford-upon-Avon before cruising on to Anne Hathaway's Cottage.

Scotland's Lochs

Distant mountains and rugged moors will be your scenery as you cruise through the magnificent surroundings along the lochs and canals in Scotland. Autumn is a spectacular time to see the forests in golden and bronze colours.

WP Exam Practice 2 Document 4

Worldwide Tours

International House Portman Square LEEDS LS5 1XX

Our ref RE/Holidays97

(Date of typing)

Mrs Valerie Rogers
The Vicarage
North Road
SPALDING
Lincs
PE11 2PN

Dear Mrs Rogers

CHRISTMAS HOLIDAY IN HARROGATE

Thank you for your recent letter enquiring about the above holiday. I understand that you would like to make a party booking for 10 people including yourself, subject to space being available. I am delighted to tell you that your party will in fact take the last places available.

Your holdiay will include arriving in Harrogate on 23 December and your hotel will be the Old Post House. There will be a welcome sherry reception in the evening followed by a talk on Harrogate.

On Christmas Eve we will have a guided tour of York Minster. There will be live musical accompaniment during dinner.

On Christmas Day you will have a celebration breakfast followed by lunch. In the afternoon you can chat over tea and Christmas cake. There will be festive games in the hotel after dinner.

On 26 December there will be a morning excursion to Ripon Cathedral and on to Fountains Abbey. The afternoon will be free for you to explore Harrogate for yourself.

On the following morning we all make for home after breakfast.

Your tour leader for the break will be Peter Williams. Peter is a very experienced leader who has led this type of group at Christmas for 3 years now.

We hope you will enjoy your traditional Christmas celebrations in Harrogate. All excursion fees are included in the holiday cost.

Yours sincerely

Ruth Edwards
Tour Organiser

cc Peter Williams
File

Copies Peter Williams ✓
File

Copies Peter Williams
File ✓

WP Exam Practice 3 Document 1

Information Sheet

Auctions

Buying at an auction is great fun. You can pick up some incredible bargains. However, you must follow a few simple rules or you may end up with more than you anticipated.

To find out where the auction rooms are, look in your local newspaper or phone book. Usually sales are held every month. General household sales are the most common. These sell everything from furniture to bric a brac. Specialist sales are held less frequently, in these you will find fine art, jewellery, silver, antiques etc.

A catalogue is usually produced for each sale. These can cost from £1 to £15 or £20 for a full-colour specialist catalogue. It is worth investing in a catalogue a few days before the sale so that you can study it at your leisure.

Viewings are held a day or two before the auction and on the day itself. It is a good idea to go along and see what is on offer. If you are planning to purchase an item, check it carefully for damage or wear and tear. Remember, once you have successfully bid for an item you have a legal obligation to purchase it.

SLS.3.2.9.7

Information Sheet 2

On the day of the sale, try to arrive a little early. Have another look at the items you wish to purchase. Decide on a price that you are willing to pay for each item.

Whatever you do, do not get carried away with the excitement of the sale and bid in excess of your reserve price.

When the bidding commences check that you can hear the auctioneer clearly. Before you enter the bidding ensure you are competing for the correct article. This sounds obvious, but you may find you end up purchasing a completely unsuitable item because you confused the catalogue numbers.

Whatever you do, do not get carried away with the excitement of the sale and bid in excess of your reserve price.

If you are fortunate enough to make a successful bid you will be expected to pay a deposit for your goods. A commission fee will also be levied. This may be approximately 10% of the bid price.

SLS.3.2.9.7

WP Exam Practice 3 Document 1 (continued)

Information Sheet 3

The full purchase price and commission fee must be paid within a specified period. This is usually 3 days. The goods must be collected straightaway or you may be liable for storage fees.

Purchasing a property through auction can often mean acquiring a property at a very realistic price. However, it can also be a gamble. The same rules apply to properties as any other goods sold through auction. Once the hammer drops you are legally obliged to complete the purchase.

> This means that if you require a mortgage this must be arranged before the auction date. Discuss this with your building society manager or other mortgage lender well in advance of the auction. You will have to pay for a surveyor's report and any mortgage arrangement fees in advance. A solicitor must also be appointed to carry out the Land Registry and local searches before the bidding commences.

SLS.3.2.9.7

4

Information Sheet

This does mean you may incur expenses of around £500 - £1000 and lose the purchase to another party. However, if you are successful, you must be able to pay the 10% deposit before leaving the auction rooms.

You will have the satisfaction of knowing that you have purchased your home at a realistic price.

Happy bargain hunting and good luck!

SLS.3.2.9.7

WP Exam Practice 3 Document 2

Auction - October

Vendor	Item	Reserve Price	Catalogue No	Estimated Price
Mr Peter Jones	Clarice Cliff Teapot	£850	CB650	£1000 - £2000
Mrs Kathy Howell	Steiff Teddy Bear	£300	TB411	£500 - £600
Ms Jenny Wood	Georgian Sewing Box	£750	MB699	£800 - £1000
Mrs Mary Brind	Victorian Pine Dresser	£890	HB111	£900 - £1200
Mr Adam More	Silver Candelabra	£1000	MB694	£1000 - £1200
Mr Roger Evans	Porcelain Figurine	£380	CB590	£300 - £450
Ms Hannah Felts	Bakelite Radio	£200	MB621	£150 - £250
Mr James Saks	Oak Sideboard	£1300	HB192	£1100 - £1300
Ms Chloe Reese	Yew Dining Table	£1500	HB184	£1500 - £2500

Items to be valued for December Sale

Item	Vendor	Notes
18th-century musical box	Raymond Withy	In fair condition, vendor says he has repaired it himself.
17th-century lacquered box	Doreen Metcalfe	Good condition.
Diamond and sapphire necklace	Vincent Bembridge	The clasp needs attention. The jewels are set in 18 carat gold.
Susie Cooper dinner service	Eleanor Grant	This was found in the attic. It is in excellent condition.
18th-century chaise longue	Helen Berry	Needs re-upholstering, some damage to frame.

WP Exam Practice 3 Document 3

October Sale

Household and General Items

The October sale will be held at 10 am on the first Monday of the month. Viewing will take place on the Friday and Saturday prior to the sale. The viewing times are 10.30 am - 6.00 pm Friday, 10.00 am - 2.00 pm Saturday. Catalogues are available at a cost of £2.50.

These monthly sales are always well-attended as local people realise they can pick up bargains for their homes. It is advisable to arrive promptly as the saleroom is often packed to capacity.

This month, items on sale include:

Dining room chairs
Dining room tables
Kitchen table
Piano
Pine dressers
Sideboards
Sofas
Wardrobes
Washing machine
Writing bureau

The reserve price of some of these items is very low. We guarantee that there will be plenty of bargains to be found.

If you cannot attend the sale in person you can still make a bid for any of the items on sale. Leave your bid and telephone number with a member of staff. They will bid on your behalf and advise you of the outcome.

Please remember, if you are successful in your bid you must be prepared to pay for and collect your purchases within 48 hours of the sale. Failure to do so will incur storage charges.

As well as the household and general items' sales we also have regular specialist auctions. These include ceramics, fine art, tapestry, special collections and silver. Details of these events are published in the specialist magazines and local newspaper.

If you would like to be informed in advance of these specialist auctions then we would be delighted to do so. Write or telephone and give details of your name and address. State which sales you are interested in. We will ensure you receive advance notification of all our events.

WP Exam Practice 3 Document 4

MEMORANDUM

To Tristan Charlton

From Miranda Alyson

Ref NYS/1/992.6.3

Date (Date of typing)

NEXT YEAR'S SALES

It really is time we planned next year's sales. I know that however well we organise the auctions our calendar is re-arranged many times, but we do need a draft outline.

I thought the best place to start would be to look at the previous few years. It may be that we should be much more analytical when organising the sales. For example, it occurred to me that it makes sense to hold sales of expensive items in November and December when customers are willing to spend. January and February are terrible months to hold auctions of fine art.

Perhaps we could meet soon to discuss this in greater detail. If possible, Wednesday of next week would be convenient. I am available all day. Let my secretary know what time would be suitable for you.

On a completely different topic, we need to appoint an auctioneer as Martin leaves the company next month. I have been searching through the computer files and found this personal quality description. I feel we could use this in the advertisement. Perhaps you would let me have your thoughts.

The suitable applicant should be unflappable, extrovert and possess a sense of humour. A love of people and fine art is an absolute must. A specialist knowledge of any area of the antiques world would be a huge advantage.

The advertisement should appear in the specialist magazines next month. If you agree to the draft then my secretary will book the advertisements straightaway. I hope we will be able to find an auctioneer as talented as Martin.

Copies Geoffrey Ferguson
File

Copies Geoffrey Ferguson
File ✓

Copies Geoffrey Ferguson ✓
File

WP Exam Practice 4 Document 1

MONTHLY BULLETIN

There is nothing that can now dampen the housing market resurgence. For months there has been an increase in the percentage of survey contributions reporting price increases with the number of sales also increasing. There is a 20% increase in the number of sales compared with last year.

Improved market conditions, together with realistic pricing has encouraged more activity in the housing market.

Confidence started to return to the market in earnest last autumn. Fears of an interest rate rise to control inflationary pressures on the economy appear to have passed by.

With spring just around the corner and confidence continuing in the housing market, we need more new properties on our books.

MARCH 1997

WP Exam Practice 4 Document 1 (continued)

MONTHLY BULLETIN

The following is a list of areas where we still have large properties for sale.

Abingdon Terrace

Claverton Down

Entry Hill Gardens

Fairfield Park

Moorfields Road

New King Street

Park Street

Royal Crescent

St Catherine's Valley

The Ley

Improved market conditions, together with realistic pricing has encouraged more activity in the housing market.

The Ley area has a substantial 4-bedroom traditional farmhouse for sale. It has 3 reception rooms and oil central heating. Situated in an unspoilt rural position. A superb family home.

An immaculate 4-bedroom semi-detached house situated in St Catherine's Valley offers a lounge, dining hall, fitted kitchen, bathroom, separate shower room and a pleasant garden. It is in the vicinity of the village and a few minutes' walk away from fields and open countryside.

MARCH 1997 2

MONTHLY BULLETIN

We now need to run a special promotion on these houses whilst the market is so buoyant. John Atkins will be responsible for this and he will let you have the details within the next week. All branches should participate in the promotion and be active in the marketing side using regular advertising. Good quality, attractive literature will encourage potential buyers.

> New housing developments continue to expand in our location. Prices range from around £40,000 to £250,000 with an average price of £60,000 for a 3-bedroom semi-detached home.

Most of these developments are within easy travelling distance of Bath and Bristol. Keep an attractive display of these developments in your showroom and have up-to-date information readily available.

Houses at the lower end of the market are priced between £44,000 and £48,500. Depending on the location, the 2-bedroomed version, complete with parking space, would include kitchen with fitted oven and hob. These are ideal for the first-time buyer market and are selling quickly.

MARCH 1997 3

WP Exam Practice 4 Document 2

NEW HOMES IN THE SOUTH WEST

Name	Address	Property Type	Completion Date	Price £
Knighton Court	Lush Valley, Barnstaple	4-bedroom houses	June 1997	150,000
Vale View	Cathedral Close, Truro	2-bedroom bungalows	October 1997	91,950
Silver Meadows	Silver Street, Devizes	Cottage style homes	March 1998	72,999
The Hedgerows	North Road, Salisbury	3-bedroom houses	September 1997	110,550
Oak Court	Moat View, Wells	Courtyard apartments	June 1998	98,999
Park Place	Cheddar View, Bristol	Community style 1-bedroom cottages	August 1997	31,500

SHOW HOME DETAILS FOR CORNWALL

Selling Agents	Development	Fixtures and accessories
Jones and Watson Edwards Property Services Vincent and Broad Group	Beacon View, St Agnes The Thornbury, Marazion Timber Touch, Truro	All show houses will be sold with fitted carpets and curtains. Fixtures include fitted wardrobes in master bedroom. Table lamps and other ancillary items can be purchased at a discount price.

WP Exam Practice 4 Document 1 (continued)

MONTHLY BULLETIN

SINCE OUR MEETING LAST MONTH IT IS APPARENT THAT A MORE PROFESSIONAL APPROACH HAS BEEN MADE TO THE RESIDENTIAL LETTINGS AND MANAGEMENT SIDE OF OUR BUSINESS. DEMAND FOR GOOD QUALITY PROPERTIES CONTINUES AND I AM SURE WE CAN BE OPTIMISTIC FOR THE FUTURE.

MARCH 1997

4

WP Exam Practice 4 Document 3

A VIEW OF ST AGNES, CORNWALL

Jones and Watson are pleased to give this brief outline of the area in which Beacon View has been developed. Local amenities include a good library, post office, two banks and a doctor's surgery. The shops in the village cater for daily provisions, clothes and footwear, pharmaceuticals, gifts and sundries. There is a frequent bus service into Truro which has an excellent shopping centre.

<u>History</u>

In the 18th and 19th centuries this was the bustling centre of a flourishing mining area. Although the majority of the mining was for tin, some copper mining also took place. St Agnes lies on a hillside and the surrounding landscape is dotted with old mine workings, tall chimneys and engine-houses.

<u>Landscape</u>

The coastline around St Agnes combines the freedom of the clifftops, with a lush agricultural interior.

Four steep-sided valleys cut into the coastline from the sea. Each valley becomes progressively more wooded as you go inland.

<u>St Agnes Beacon</u>

The Beacon is like a great island of sedimentary rock standing above the granite. Paths flanked by gorse and heather lead to the summit, which is over 600 feet above sea level. A view from here gives a 30-mile panoramic sweep of the Atlantic coast.

Recreational features include a nearby golf course, horse riding, clay pigeon shooting and tennis. There are also two playing fields, one with a football pitch plus play equipment.

Village life can be fun. You will be able to take an active part in some of the Annual Events, namely the May Ball or Carnival Week in August.

WP Exam Practice 4 Document 4

MEMORANDUM

To Clare Young

From John Atkins

Ref HB/PL/1997

Date (Date of typing)

SPRING SPECIAL PROMOTION

At the March monthly meeting I was asked to co-ordinate a special promotion for selling some of the larger properties we still have on our books. I would like you to prepare your branch's information for me. Refer any queries you may have to my secretary, Rebecca Morris.

Please include the following points in your reply.

1 How long the property has been on your books and how many potential buyers have viewed it in the last two months.
2 The asking price and whether you think this is realistic. If the price has been dropped since the original one was fixed, let me know if you think it feasible to lower it again.
3 A full description of the property including outbuildings, car parking areas and gardens.
4 <u>What amenities are in the area for children.</u> You should include schools in this section too. Larger properties are usually bought as family homes and we need to make this a high priority selling point.

I would like to see the house in St Catherine's Valley sold as little interest has apparently been shown in it over the last year.

New photographs of the properties will be taken by Homes in Camera, and when I have the above information from all branches in the South West, I will endeavour to publish an attractive fact sheet for distribution.

cc Rebecca Morris
File

cc Rebecca Morris ✓
File

cc Rebecca Morris
File ✓

WP Exam Practice 5 Document 1

GOVERNING BODY

School Governing Body

The governing body of each local education authority maintained school is made up of a number of representatives from the school, parents and the local community.

The body has a number of duties as well as legal responsibilities. The main duties are listed below.

1 Establish the aims and policies of the school and how the required educational standards can be met

2 Deciding how the school should be run

3 Assisting the staff to draw up the school development plan

4 Deciding how to spend the school budget in the most efficient way

5 Ensuring the National Curriculum and religious education are taught

6 Appointing a head teacher

7 Appointing, supporting, promoting and disciplining other staff

8 Acting as a link between the school and the local community

9 Drawing up an action plan and monitoring its progress

Information Sheet 3

2

GOVERNING BODY

<u>Becoming a School Governor</u>

Each school needs enthusiastic, motivated people who are interested in the education of young people. There are a number of parent governors on the governing body of each school.

When a vacancy arises, you can put yourself forward for election. Two parents of children at the school must support your application. If more than one parent wishes to become a governor, an election will be held. Usually, you can write a short paragraph about yourself and your suitability to hold office. Parents are then asked to vote.

For only a few hours each week, you can make a big contribution to the running of your child's school, and help your local community.

Information Sheet 3

WP Exam Practice 5 Document 1 (continued)

3

GOVERNING BODY

<u>What Qualifications Do I Need?</u>

Formal qualifications are not necessary, nor do you need to have any specialist knowledge of education. You will still be able to make a valid contribution to the running of a school. The head teacher and staff will be able to advise you on matters concerning education. You may be able to use your own areas of expertise in helping the school make important decisions.

> What you do need is enthusiasm, loyalty and some spare time. It helps if you are a good listener. You will then be able to collect many different views on school issues. This will enable you to make informed decisions.

Team working is another important skill. The governing body must work well together and have the school's best interests at heart. Although the governing body has many duties and responsibilities, no individual governor has any powers within the school.

Information Sheet 3

4

GOVERNING BODY

<u>How much time is involved?</u>

The full governing body usually meets at least twice a term. However, Committees dealing with specialised areas such as:

curriculum

finance

lettings

marketing

personnel

premises

school development

are formed and you may be expected to sit on one or two of these.

As well as attending meetings you may have to read reports and Government papers and visit the school from time to time. This may not take as much time as it first appears. You do however need to make a commitment to the school and be prepared to attend meetings regularly.

For only a few hours each week, you can make a big contribution to the running of your child's school, and help your local community.

Information Sheet 3

WP Exam Practice 5 Document 3

<u>Clerk to the Governors</u>

Parker Primary School is looking to appoint a new clerk to the governing body. The position would suit someone with school-age children as all committee meetings are held in the evenings. Parker Primary School would especially welcome applications from parents at the school.

The most suitable candidate will have secretarial skills, especially in word processing and general presentation of documents. Shorthand speed would be advantageous as minuting meetings will be the main duty.

As well as secretarial skills, the applicant must be enthusiastic, loyal and above all, discreet. As clerk to the governing body, the post-holder will have access to a great deal of confidential information.

The duties will include attending and minuting meetings which will involve approximately six evenings per academic term. Preparing agendas and notices, typing up minutes and distributing to the governing body will also be part of these duties.

Governors' newsletters which go out to parents each term are produced and designed by the clerk. Desktop publishing skills would be an advantage.

The post-holder will also be required to deal with the routine correspondence of the governors. It is anticipated that this should not take longer than 2-3 hours per week. Liaising with the local education authority's link governor committee will also form part of the post.

Training is given and the clerk will have the opportunity to attend courses organised by the local education authority.

An honorarium of approximately £1500 - £2000 will be paid each academic year. This is reviewed each academic year.

If you are interested in holding this very challenging position, please contact Gerry Miles, the head teacher.

WP Exam Practice 5 Document 2

Parker Primary School - Governing Body

Name	Address	Type of Governor	Start Date	Finish Date
Mrs S Davison	10 Bath Street, LEEDS LS1 6BY	Parent	10.02.97	10.02.01
Mrs P Allen	20 Burnham Road, LEEDS LS2 4HK	Co-opted	24.06.95	24.06.99
Mr K Morrison	71 Mount Road, LEEDS LS8 7SL	Teacher	01.11.94	01.11.98
Mrs B Smedley	3 Magdalen Avenue, LEEDS LS1 4NE	LEA	23.09.94	23.09.98
Ms H Lawson	92 Lillie Road, LEEDS, LS1 7TC	LEA	16.04.96	16.04.00
Ms L Norwood	16 Coromandel Heights, LEEDS LS1 8IL	LEA	05.10.95	05.10.99
Revd D Vincent	The Rectory, Ball Street, LEEDS LS1 3WP	Parent	17.01.96	17.01.00
Dr S Hansome	30 Audley Park, LEEDS LS2 7GJ	Co-opted	30.10.94	30.10.98
Mrs K Booth	3 Rosslyn Way, LEEDS LS7 6AP	Parent	28.03.96	23.03.00
Mr N Ramsey	1 Bellotts Road, LEEDS LS1 9QX	Co-opted	05.05.95	05.05.99
Mrs P Mulligan	72 Coronation Avenue, LEEDS LS1 8KJ	Parent	12.09.96	12.09.00
Mr G Miles	34 Newbridge Hill, LEEDS LS1 2BU	Head	06.09.94	06.09.98

Committee Members

Committee	Responsibilities	Chairperson
Curriculum	To oversee the delivery of the National Curriculum. To ensure that a scheme of work and related resources are up to date and readily available.	Mr K Morrison
Premises	To oversee the maintenance of the school environment. To advise on safety. To advise on lettings policy.	Revd D Vincent
Personnel	To appoint, support, promote staff including head teacher. To follow disciplinary procedures where necessary.	Mrs P Allen
Finance	To manage school budget and advise where necessary.	Dr S Hansome

WP Exam Practice 5 Document 4

Parker
Primary
School

Kingston Avenue
LEEDS
LS40 3QL

Our Ref LK/SD/431.6

(Date of typing)

Mrs S Davison
10 Bath Street
LEEDS
LS1 6BY

Dear Mrs Davison

Parent Governor Election

As returning officer I am pleased to inform you that you have been successful in the above election for parent governor. I am sure you will find the experience both interesting and enjoyable.

The Governing Body of Parker Primary School consists of 12 members. This number is dictated by the number of pupils registered. The governors are made up of a variety of people, as set out in Government guidelines.

Parent governors make up four of the members, three people can be appointed by the local education authority. These generally represent local political parties. A teacher representative must also be appointed. The head teacher may choose whether they wish to be a member of the Governing Body. However, even if the head teacher decides not to be a governor, their attendance at meetings is necessary.

The Body may have up to four co-opted members. These are appointed by the Body and are usually local people who have an interest in the school. They may represent the local business community.

The Governing Body is divided into four committees: these are premises, finance, personnel and curriculum. They meet on a regular basis, approximately three times each term. Reports are made from each committee to the full Governing Body which meets at least twice each term.

I am enclosing some information on the school governing body which I hope you will find interesting and useful.

2

The next meeting of the governing body is on the 28th of next month. I look forward to seeing you then. However, if you would like to discuss your new role further, please contact me.

Yours sincerely

Gerry Miles
Head teacher

Enc

Copies Chair of Governors
File

Copies Chair of Governors
File ✓

Copies Chair of Governors ✓
File

WP Exam Practice 6 Document 1

RELAXING HOBBIES

The pace of life today is very stressful. It is very important to use free time sensibly and follow a hobby that will give the mind and body complete relaxation.

Art, whether painting, sketching or calligraphy, is a wonderful way to relax. We have the course to suit your individual need and you will find them all described in our part-time programme for this current academic year.

You may be interested in our new weekend workshop on handling conflict with creativity. Relationships in the home or at work can be damaged by conflict. This workshop uses art, visualisation and role play to identify needs and communicate feelings of anger or hurt.

ART COURSES

RELAXING HOBBIES

The course is suitable for people who are interested in personal growth and it requires no previous art skills. You will need to bring with you:

Adhesive tape

Cartridge paper

Clipboard

Collage materials

Crayons

Pencils

Pens

Scissors

Sketch pad

> Many people have an urge to produce water-colours. They do not realise that a good background in the knowledge of drawing is imperative for final success. Many prospective students are impatient and fail to understand the need for discipline and the importance of drawing skills.

Remember, you need confidence to be able to draw.

ART COURSES 2

WP Exam Practice 6 Document 1 (continued)

RELAXING HOBBIES

If you are a beginner you can join a group and be shown how to draw a variety of objects, also simple perspective.

Progression will take place on to the opportunity of drawing the human form as well as proportion. Portraiture will be included in this course. The group usually consists of people of all ages and abilities.

If you have already acquired the expertise necessary in drawing forms, you may wish to portray your drawing in terms of water-colour. The more practice you have had with your pencil, the more freely you will be able to express yourself with the brush.

THERE ARE A NUMBER OF COURSES FOR YOU TO CHOOSE FROM. WE HAVE A STRUCTURED COURSE ON COLOUR THEORY AND TECHNIQUES OF WATER-COLOUR. OUR SYLLABUS ALLOWS FOR FLEXIBILITY AND DOES NOT INCLUDE METHODICALLY PRESCRIBED EXERCISES. ROOM MUST ALWAYS BE LEFT FOR SELF EXPRESSION.

ART COURSES 3

RELAXING HOBBIES

As soon as an idea for a painting is formalised in your mind, set it down in sketch form. Spontaneous paintings are often the result of this form of work.

After attending our courses you will have the background knowledge necessary for you to participate further on your own in your chosen art area. If you wish to enter for a qualification, a GCSE or A-level course will be your next move.

Remember, you need confidence to be able to draw.

ART COURSES 4

WP Exam Practice 6 Document 3

CALLIGRAPHY FOR ALL

From an introduction to the foundation hand and capitals to italic style and colour calligraphy, this is a hobby everyone can enjoy. Most courses are for a 10 week block and include the following themes.

<u>Illuminated Alphabets</u>

Alphabets that will inspire everyone to design and decorate capital letters. Each alphabet will have basic design instructions together with ideas for variations.

Whether you are interpreting the words of a text or perhaps decorating a name, your finished piece of work should be harmonious and pleasing to the eye.

<u>Borders with Flowers</u>

Artists have used plants as a source of inspiration for centuries. Delicate flower heads, stems and leaves can be safely entwined round any awkward gap or corner. Flowers can be adapted in a variety of ways. You can use a free-flowing pattern which can be lengthened or shortened as necessary.

For a rose border you can decorate the initial letter, paint the inside roses in a water-colour and the bordering branches in a gouache.

<u>Colour Style</u>

Although some traditional approaches demand the use of black ink, who can resist colour? Colour makes calligraphy attractive, more effective and memorable.

A suitable work surface and a comfortable working position are essential for calligraphy and illumination. Use a slanting work surface. A good comfortable chair that is the right height for you will help to prevent backache.

A good quality cartridge paper is ideal for beginners. A set of pencils from the H range and quill, reed and metal-nibbed pens are all essential.

WP Exam Practice 6 Document 2

CREATIVITY COURSES

Title	Leader	Course Code	Fee Code	Course Duration	Commencement Date
Art - Painting Flowers	Mary Jackson	B011/03	JJ	18 weeks	15 September
Life Drawing	John Watson	B003/05	KK	20 weeks	17 September
Calligraphy - Beginners	Mavis Stanton	C015/04	AB	10 weeks	6 October
Cloth Sculpture	Anne Hall	C002/10	AC	12 weeks	7 October
Embroidered Boxes	Susan Netherby	C009/01	AD	6 weeks	10 November
Dressmaking	Karen Field	C007/07	AE	20 weeks	18 September

WEEKEND COURSES

Subject	Description	Where	When
Bead Work	How to use beads in embroidery, patchwork and quilting.	Main College	14 and 15 June
Stained Glass	Use traditional glass and lead methods to design and make a small glass panel.	West Hall Church	12 and 13 July
Book Covers	Cover a special book using either plain or patterned fabric.	College Annexe	2 and 3 August

WP Exam Practice 6 Document 4

Minster College of Art

Knaresborough Road
YORK
YO2 9BW

Our ref BW/587

(Date of typing)

Mrs Dorothy Reed
Park View House
31 North Road
WAKEFIELD
WF1 4HL

Dear Mrs Reed

CREATIVE STUDIES - STAINED GLASS WEEKEND

Thank you for your letter of enquiry concerning the above course. I am pleased to confirm the weekend will be led by Joanne Chambers and will take place in West Hall Church.

You will have the whole weekend in which to design and make your own small stained glass panel. Traditional glass methods will be used and no previous experience is necessary.

You will be able to purchase the basic tools necessary at a cost of approximately £17.50. In addition to this there will be a charge of £12.50 for materials. The course fee will be £30 for the whole weekend.

Would you please pay the full amount of £60 at the time of your application. We accept payment by credit card, cash or cheque. Cheques should be made payable to the college with your name and address on the back.

You may enrol in person or by post. The college reception office is open from 9 am to 4 pm on Monday to Friday. Complete the booking form at the back of your prospectus if you would like to enrol by post.

If you wish to book a place by telephone you will need to have your credit card details, course code and title etc. We will also accept bookings by fax provided you have given your credit card details and authorisation.

Yours sincerely

Barbara Watson
Course Co-ordinator

cc Joanne Chambers
File

cc Joanne Chambers
File ✓

cc Joanne Chambers ✓
File